The IE

Choice in Welfare No.33

Charles Murray and the Underclass: The Developing Debate

Charles Murray

commentaries

Ruth Lister (Editor)
Frank Field MP
Joan C. Brown
Alan Walker
Nicholas Deakin

Pete Alcock
Miriam David
Melanie Phillips
Sue

A Statist

Alan B

IEA Health and Welfare Unit
in association with *The Sunday Times*
London, 1996

First published November 1996
Third Impression, June 1999

The IEA Health and Welfare Unit
2 Lord North St
London SW1P 3LB

ISBN 0-255 36391-5

ISSN 1362-9565

Typeset by the IEA Health and Welfare Unit
in New Century Schoolbook 10 on 11 point
Printed in Great Britain by
Hartington Fine Arts Ltd, Lancing, West Sussex

Contents

Foreword

This publication brings together Charles Murray's two major essays on the British Underclass. Part 1 reproduces *The Emerging British Underclass* originally published by the IEA in 1990 following its earlier appearance in the *Sunday Times Magazine*. The commentaries by Frank Field, Joan C. Brown, Alan Walker and Nicholas Deakin are also reprinted.

Part 2 reprints Charles Murray's follow-up essay, *Underclass: The Crisis Deepens* which was first published in September 1994 following its appearance in *The Sunday Times* in May of that year. Four commentaries by Pete Alcock, Miriam David, Melanie Phillips and Sue Slipman are also reproduced.

This edition benefits from a new introduction by Professor Ruth Lister and a statistical update by Alan Buckingham.

David G. Green

The Authors

Charles Murray is the author of *Losing Ground: American Social Policy 1950-1980*, 1984; *In Pursuit of Happiness and Good Government*, 1988; *The Emerging British Underclass*, 1990; and, with Richard Herrnstein, *The Bell Curve: Intelligence and Class Structure in American Life*, 1994. He is the Bradley Fellow at the American Enterprise Institute, a public policy research institute in Washington, DC.

Pete Alcock is Professor of Social Policy at Sheffield Hallam University. He has written widely in the area of poverty, social security and anti-poverty policy and is the author of *Understanding Poverty* and *Social Poverty in Britain*. His major research interests are in the field of local anti-poverty action and welfare rights. Professor Alcock is currently the Chair of the Social Policy Association, and he is a member of the Editorial Boards of *Journal of Social Policy* and *Benefits*.

Joan C. Brown is an independent researcher in social policy and was formerly employed as a Senior Research Fellow at the Policy Studies Institute. Her principal interests are social security and poverty, both in the UK and in the European Community. Earlier in her career she worked in Australia and Canada and she retains an interest in developments in these countries.

While at the Policy Studies Institute, Joan Brown had a series of studies published on issues of family income support, disability income and occupational benefits. Since 1988, her published studies have included: *In Search of a Policy: the Rationale for Social Security Provision for One-Parent Families*, 1988; *Child Benefit: Investing in the Future*, 1988; a study for the Social Security Advisory Committee entitled *Why Don't They Go to Work? Mothers on Benefit*, 1989; and *Victims or Villains? Social Security Benefits in Unemployment*, 1990.

Alan Buckingham was born in 1969. The son of a factory worker, his formative years were spent living on a council housing estate in close proximity to members of the 'underclass'. He gained a first-class honours degree in Sociology at the University of Sussex in 1994 and is now completing his PhD. under the supervision of Professor Peter Saunders. His research, utilising a study of 17,000 men and women, is examining how and why people become part of the underclass.

Miriam David is Professor of Social Sciences at South Bank University, Director of the Social Sciences Research Centre and also Head of Research and Vice Chair of the University's Research Committee. She is also visiting Professorial Fellow at the University of London Institute of Education. Her books include *Parents, Gender and Educational Reform*, Polity Press, 1993 and with Drs Rosalind Edwards, Mary Hughes and Jane Ribbens, *Mothers and Education: Inside Out?*, Macmillan, 1993. She is also currently the co-editor, with Dr Dulcie Groves, of the *Journal of Social Policy*, published by Cambridge University Press.

Nicholas Deakin has been Professor of Social Policy and Administration at Birmingham University since 1980. Previously he worked as a civil servant and then on a research programme in race relations funded by the Nuffield Foundation. After spending three years in the late 1960s researching and teaching at Sussex University, he went back to work in government, where he served as Head of the Central Policy Unit at the GLC.

Professor Deakin has published numerous books and articles on race relations, urban policy, new towns and voluntary action. His most recent publications are *The Politics of Welfare,* 1994 and *Consuming Public Services,* (with A.W. Wright and others) 1990, and *The Enterprise Culture and the Inner Cities*, (with John Edwards), 1992. He chaired the Independent Inquiry on the Voluntary Sector in England which reported in 1996.

Frank Field has been the Labour Member of Parliament for Birkenhead since 1979. He has been a front-bench spokesman on education and social security, chairman of the Commons Social Services Select Committee and is currently the chairman of the Social Security Select Committee. Recent publications include: *Losing Out: the Emergence of Britain's Underclass*, and *An Agenda for Britain*.

Other Institute of Community Studies publications allied to *How To Pay For the Future* are: Field, F., *Making Welfare Work*, 1995 (out of print); Field, F., Halligan, L. and Owen, M., *Europe Isn't Working*, 1994; and Field, F. and Owen, M., *Beyond Punishment: Hard Choices on the Road to Full Employability*, 1994.

Ruth Lister is Professor of Social Policy at Loughborough University. She has published and spoken widely in the areas of poverty, income maintenance and women's welfare. Her publications include: *The Exclusive Society: Citizenship and the Poor*, CPAG, 1990 and *Women's Economic Dependency and Social Security*, Equal Opportunities Commission, 1992. Her latest book, *Citizenship: Feminist Perspectives* is due to be published by Macmillan in 1997. She is a former Director of the Child Poverty Action Group and served on the Commission on Social Justice.

Melanie Phillips is a columnist for *The Observer* who writes about social issues and political culture. She is the author of *Divided House*, a study of women at Westminster, and co-author with Dr John Dawson of *Doctors' Dilemmas,* a primer on medical ethics. Her controversial new book, *All Must Have Prizes* (Little Brown) charts the disastrous effects of our culture of individualism upon the education system and the moral order.

Sue Slipman is the Director of the Gas Consumers' Council and a member of the Advisory Committee on Women's Issues to the Secretary of State at the Department of Employment. She was the Director of the National Council for One Parent Families from 1985-1995, and is Chair of the Advice Guidance Counselling and Psychotherapy Lead Body.

Alan Walker is Professor of Social Policy at the University of Sheffield. He has taught at the University of Sheffield since 1977 and has held the Chair of Social Policy since 1985.

Professor Walker is sole author, co-author, or editor of more than fifteen books, including *Unqualified and Underemployed,* 1982; *Social Planning,* 1984; *Ageing and Social Policy,* (ed. with C. Phillipson) 1986; *After Redundancy,* (with I. Noble and J. Westergaard) 1989; *The New Generational Contract*, 1996 and *Ageing Europe* (with T. Maltby), 1996. He has also contributed numerous articles and chapters to learned journals and edited books in social policy and social gerontology. He is currently engaged in two major research studies—one is on the employment of older workers in Europe and the other is on care for older people with learning difficulties.

Introduction: In Search of the 'Underclass'

Ruth Lister

Introduction

IN 1989 Charles Murray visited Britain in search of the 'underclass', courtesy of *The Sunday Times*. Four years later he returned to warn that the crisis of the 'underclass' was deepening.[1] The two essays which Murray wrote are brought together here, in one volume, together with a number of critical commentaries and a rejoinder from Murray to some of them. Whereas Murray's first essay discusses the concept of an 'underclass' in fairly general terms, relating it to trends in 'illegitimacy', crime and unemployment, the second is primarily pre-occupied with 'illegitimacy', marriage and the state of the British family. The commentaries by Joan Brown, Miriam David and Sue Slipman are unequivocally critical of Murray's interpretation of family trends; Melanie Phillips (p. 157), shares Murray's concern about the 'collapse of the family' but disputes his analysis of the causes and his policy prescriptions. The commentaries by Alan Walker, Nicholas Deakin and Pete Alcock provide a more broad-based critique of Murray's conceptualisation of an 'underclass' whilst Frank Field, who himself uses the term, provides a different interpretation of its nature to that of Murray. A new appendix is provided by Alan Buckingham who both updates and supplements Murray's data and analysis.

This new Introduction[2] is written from the perspective of a long-standing critic of the use of the term 'underclass' on both academic and political grounds. It is for this reason that the word 'underclass' appears here in inverted commas. However, whatever one's views about the concept, it clearly cannot be ignored as it has become a key word in the British political, academic and media lexicon, in part, at least, because of Murray's two essays. The purpose of this Introduction is not to re-run the debates between Murray and his critics in the later pages, although inevitably there will be a degree of overlap. Instead, its main focus will be the concept of the 'underclass' itself: the different ways it is understood, defined and used and their academic and political implications.

Identifying the 'Underclass': Origins

The concept of the 'underclass' does not originate with Murray, nor do all who deploy it share Murray's understanding of its nature and causes.[3] The term was coined in the US and was popularised there in the early 1980s by the journalist Ken Auletta who emphasised the behaviour and values of those deemed to be members of the 'underclass', though without claiming that these were necessarily the cause of their plight. The concept was also propagated by William Julius Wilson, former president of the American Sociological Association. Wilson, however, emphasised the structural labour market position rather than the behaviour of the 'underclass' and has subsequently raised a question mark over the term's usage, particularly in the European context.

Wilson's work, which highlighted the position of urban blacks, also underlines the racialised nature of the 'underclass' debate in the US. In Britain, earlier usage of the term in the 1970s tended also to focus on the racial dimension as a way of demonstrating the impact of discriminatory employment and housing policies on minority ethnic groups. In an essay which helped to popularise the notion of an 'underclass' in Britain, Ralf (now Lord) Dahrendorf likewise emphasises that it is 'a phenomenon of race' here as well as the US. From a different political perspective, A. Sivanandan has attacked the creation of an 'underclass' in Western Europe as well as the US, the result, he contends, of a 'symbiosis between racism and poverty' under multinational capitalism.[4] Robert Moore, too, has suggested that, despite his own misgivings, a collective term such as the 'underclass' may be needed to refer to that group of marginalised migrant workers, refugees and asylum seekers, inner city ethnic minority populations and the very poorest who 'typically have little or no control over goods and skills either within or outside a given economic order'.[5] However, both Murray and Field in this volume explicitly dispute a racial connotation in the British context where the black population is much smaller than in the US.[6]

Field's own exposition of the emergence of a British 'underclass', *Losing Out*, identifies four main 'forces of expulsion'—unemployment, widening class differences, the exclusion of the very poorest from rapidly rising living standards, and a hardening of public attitudes—as having created an 'underclass', separated from the rest of society 'in terms of income, life chances and political aspirations'.

This process of exclusion he conceptualises as 'the loss of a comprehensive approach to citizenship'.[7] As Field's contribution to this volume emphasises, his starting point is the structural causes of an 'underclass' in contrast to Murray's analysis which focuses on behaviour as both its cause and defining characteristic. It is this association between an 'underclass' and the behaviour of its members which has prompted much of the controversy around the work of Murray and others who subscribe to his 'underclass' thesis. It is an association with long historical antecedents and the debate about the role of behaviour in causing poverty has surfaced in various guises over the years.[8]

Defining the 'Underclass': An Elastic Concept

Christopher Jencks has described how, in the US, the search for a definition of the 'underclass' followed its media popularisation and appeal:

> It focuses attention on the basement of the American social system (those who are 'under' the rest of us), without specifying what the inhabitants of this dark region have in common. Once the term entered the vernacular, however, journalists and policymakers inevitably began asking social scientists how large it was and why it was growing. Since neither journalists nor policy analysts had a clear idea what they meant by the underclass, social scientists had to make up their own definitions. We now have nearly a dozen of these definitions, each yielding a different picture of how big the underclass is and who its members are... It soon became clear, however, that those who talked about the underclass had something more in mind than just persistent poverty. The term underclass, with its echoes of the underworld, conjures up sin, or at least unorthodox behaviour. Low income may be a necessary condition for membership in such a class, but it is not sufficient.[9]

He suggests that three different kinds of 'underclass' are, in fact, being talked about: an economic (those of working age unable to get steady work); a moral (those with deviant behavioural norms) and an educational (those lacking in cultural and social skills).

Seven years later there is still no single agreed definition of the 'underclass' and different definitions tend to reflect whether the definer subscribes to a structural or behavioural/cultural explanation of its causes. Definitions then get tangled up with explanations and with the highly charged political interpretations that permeate the debate around an 'underclass'. This is exemplified by Murray's behavioural definition which, as he emphasises in this volume, refers not to 'degree of poverty, but to a type of poverty'. In a Foreword to the first edition of Murray's essay, David Green spells out this type of poverty: 'those distinguished by their undesirable behaviour, including drug-taking, crime, illegitimacy, failure to hold down a job, truancy from school and casual violence' (p. 19).

In his Update Buckingham proposes therefore, as a less ambiguous definition of the underclass, 'dependency on the state' which, in turn, is characterised in terms of benefit receipt and residence in public housing and the regulation of life chances this involves. Leaving aside the pejorative connotations of the notion of welfare dependency, which itself is often associated with 'behavioural poverty', how useful is this definition in distinguishing an 'underclass' from the wider group of those in poverty?

Certainly it has the advantage that it is, at first sight, easily operationisable. But simply to define everyone either in receipt of state benefits or in public housing as a member of the 'underclass' raises questions both about some of those included and some of those excluded by the definition. Many people are reliant on benefits for only a short time; on this definition they would appear automatically to become members of an 'underclass' for the duration of their benefit receipt. Others are only able to afford low paid work by topping it up with means-tested benefits; are they in or out of the 'underclass'? Similarly, are full time workers living in council housing by definition members of the 'underclass'? And are home-owners reliant on income support in or out? Nor is the position of those outside the labour market—the chronically sick and those of pension age—clear. Conversely, on this definition a long-term homeless person not receiving any state benefits but getting by on begging would not be a member of the 'underclass'. What these questions illustrate is the difficulty of using an administrative criterion as the basis of a sociological definition. Indeed, Buckingham himself narrows it down in a footnote for the purposes of his analysis of 33-year-olds in the National Child Development Study to those out of the labour force for a total of at least 2.5 years and who have been on benefit and living in a council house (excluding those registered disabled).

A similar lack of clarity underlies Field's account of the 'underclass' which, in the absence of an explicit definition, incorporates three groups—very frail elderly pensioners, lone parents on welfare and the long term unemployed—without making clear what it is that distinguishes them as members of an 'underclass' from other potentially long-term benefit recipients such as chronically sick or severely disabled people. Alternatively, David Willetts, now a Conservative MP, suggests that 'the simplest definition of the "underclass" is long-term or frequent claimants of income support', which would include what he identifies as the three key groups of 'the long-term unemployed, unskilled workers in erratic employment and younger single mothers'.[10]

A rather more sophisticated attempt at defining the 'underclass' in terms of benefit receipt is provided by W.G. Runciman who, in the context of a class analysis, defines the 'underclass' as those beneath the working classes 'whose roles place them more or less permanently at the economic level where benefits are paid by the state to those unable to participate in the labour market at all'.[11] Here it is not simply benefit receipt which defines the 'underclass' but also their exclusion from the labour market on a more or less permanent basis.[12]

Drawing on Runciman's class-based approach, David J. Smith of the Policy Studies Institute (PSI) provides an alternative structural definition of the 'underclass' which detaches it from benefit receipt. In his 'minimalist' approach, 'the underclass are those who fall outside this class schema, because they belong to family units having no stable relationship at all with the "mode of production"—with legitimate gainful employment'.[13] Some degree of stability of membership is integral to this definition. Smith explicitly distinguishes between his structural definition of the 'underclass' and questions of existence, explanation, composition, behavioural and cultural characteristics and effect which are left open to be answered by empirical research. Thus, the 'underclass' is defined purely and simply in terms of relationship to the labour market.

Relationship to the labour market also forms the basis of the structural definitions of the 'underclass' deployed in the US by sociologists such as Wilson, although there is a tendency for behavioural characteristics also to creep in. Thus, for instance, in his most important work Wilson defines the 'underclass' as:

> that heterogeneous grouping of families and individuals who are outside the mainstream of the American occupational system. Included... are individuals who lack training and skills and either experience long-term unemployment or are not members of the labor force, individuals who are

engaged in street crime and other forms of aberrant behaviour, and families that experience long-term spells of poverty and/or welfare dependency.[14]

However, according to William R. Prosser, Wilson now subscribes to a definition developed by Martha Van Haitsma in which the 'underclass' are 'those persons who are weakly connected to the formal labor force and whose social context tends to maintain or further weaken this attachment' so that structural factors are either reinforced or counteracted by the cultural factors of social context.[15]

Prosser, a senior policy adviser in the Bush administration, concludes his review of the state of the debate and the evidence in the US with the observation that, despite the volume of research undertaken 'we still do not have agreement on what we mean by the underclass, much less what factors are associated with its growth'.[16] Indeed, Murray himself concedes that it is a waste of time trying to count the 'underclass' as 'it all depends on how one defines its membership... The size of the underclass can be made to look huge or insignificant, depending on what one wants the answer to be' (p. 41). If, as we have seen and as Murray himself acknowledges, definitions of the 'underclass' are so elastic, it must raise questions about its validity and usefulness as a sociological concept. This conclusion is reinforced by an examination of relevant research undertaken in the UK.

Desperately Seeking the 'Underclass': the Research Evidence

Smith's 'minimalist' structural definition of the 'underclass' provides the basis for an attempt by Nick Buck, in a collection of essays edited by Smith for the PSI, to ascertain whether it is possible to identify such a group, with no stable relationship to the labour market, in Britain. Although his analysis of long-term unemployment suggests at first sight that it is possible to identify such a group, constituting around five per cent of the population in 1979 and ten per cent in 1986, he warns that, without life-history data, it is difficult to reach any firm conclusions:

> The problem is that even when we are speaking of long-term unemployment we do not have evidence that this is really persistent over an entire non-working life. For the vast majority of the long-term unemployed in the mid-1980s unemployment came as a major

interruption to a working life and was not a normal condition. They were not so much members of a stable underclass as unstable members of the working class.[17]

Research into lone parenthood suggests that 'a typical spell is three and a half years, and though there is quite a wide dispersion around this median, relatively few go the distance. Those who do tend to be those better able to look after themselves. Multiple spells of lone parenthood are quite rare'.[18] Durations of lone parenthood are, typically, no longer for single than divorced mothers.[19] Ford et al note that:

> more are in paid work than is commonly supposed. Half of lone parents are economically active, that is working or looking for work. Like a lot of other people, they have found work harder to come by in the early 1990s, so seven per cent are keen to work but are 'unemployed and seeking work'. Only a quarter work full-time but this is exactly the same proportion as married women with dependent children who work full-time.[20]

Like other researchers they also identify the availability of child care as a key factor in determining whether lone mothers are able to undertake paid employment. The unavailability of affordable child care is an important reason why lone mothers, who are less likely to have access to informal free sources of childcare,[21] are likely to be reliant on income support for longer than other groups. Overall, analysis of the dynamics of benefit receipt suggests that 'the majority of income support recipients come and go quickly while a minority of long term recipients tends to accumulate in the system'.[22] More generally, an analysis of panel data, which permits the tracking of incomes over time, 'indicates that there is not a single homogeneous group who are "the poor" and whose lot is permanently to remain poor. Rather, fluctuations in personal circumstances lead to considerable variations in living standards even from one year to the next'.[23]

In the PSI volume Anthony Heath analyses data on attitudes towards family life and paid employment and concludes that there is no evidence of a 'culture of dependency' amongst members of the 'underclass', operationally defined as family units where neither partner (in the case of couples) is currently in paid employment and where a member has been in receipt of social assistance in the previous five years.

Duncan Gallie adopts a similar approach in analysing attitudes towards work amongst those studied in six local labour markets as part of the ESRC Social Change and Economic Life Initiative. He found little support for the notion of an 'underclass' with a separate sub-culture amongst the long-term unemployed. Instead, 'the evidence pointed very consistently to the conclusion that attitudes to work of the long-term unemployed are not distinctive and are not an important factor accounting for people's vulnerability to unemployment'. He concludes that 'overall, analyses of the unemployed in terms of the emergence of an underclass would appear to obscure rather than to clarify the major determinants and implications of unemployment'.[24]

Smaller scale qualitative studies of poor families living on benefit have also questioned the existence of an 'underclass' in the sense of a group with a distinct sub-culture. Jonathan Bradshaw and Hilary Holmes, for instance, dispute the notion of an 'underclass', arguing that the families they studied 'are just the same people as the rest of our population, with the same culture and aspirations, but with simply too little money to be able to share in the activities and possessions of everyday life with the rest of the population'.[25] More recently, Elaine Kempson concludes from her review of 31 research studies supported by the Joseph Rowntree Foundation that:

> people who live on low incomes are not an underclass. They have aspirations just like others in society: they want a job; a decent home; and an income that is enough to pay the bills with a little to spare. But social and economic changes that have benefited the majority of the population, increasing their incomes and their standard of living, have made life more difficult for a growing minority, whose fairly modest aspirations are often beyond their reach.[26]

Of course, there have always been some people—poor or otherwise—who meet the criteria ascribed to the 'underclass' but it is yet to be shown that they constitute a separate class with a separate set of values. The conclusion reached by Smith in his PSI report is that 'the theory that an underclass is being created as a result of spontaneous cultural change, or in response to the structure of the social security system, is in conflict with a considerable weight of evidence'. Nevertheless, he does envisage a possible scenario in ten to twenty years time when persistent high-long term unemployment, concentrated amongst particular families and groups, could lead to the development of an increasingly separate culture and way of life as a means of adaptation. Thus, he argues 'it has not yet been shown that the underclass is a coherent explanatory idea in Britain, but it may yet turn out to be a good way of explaining the society that will be created by present conditions if they persist'.[27]

In speculating about the possible cultural adaptation of those more or less permanently excluded from the labour market, Smith is implicitly departing from his strictly structural definition of the 'underclass'. This, I would suggest, reflects the way in which the discourse of the 'underclass' is shaped by the assumptions of those like Murray who subscribe to cultural or behavioural definitions and explanations so that it is very difficult to quarantine attempts at more neutral accounts such as Smith's from their influence.[28]

Talking about the 'Underclass': Language and Politics.

The power of this discourse and of the language it uses is not to be underestimated. Even some commentators who do not subscribe to Murray's thesis acknowledge that the notion of an 'underclass' has served as a 'powerful tool of political rhetoric for both left and right'.[29] In the US, Jencks, whilst counselling against its use by social scientists because of its ambiguity, nonetheless suggests that it does 'seem to be a good formula for drawing attention to problems that American society has largely ignored since the mid-1970s'. As such it could serve 'an extraordinarily useful purpose'.[30]

Similarly, in the UK, Fred Robinson and Nicky Gregson argue that it is:

> necessary to appreciate that powerful words can be used effectively to present important and powerful messages. There is no doubt that a careful use of the underclass as a term and concept can be very effective. It can serve to highlight key problems: the fact of increasing social polarisation; the entrapment of the poorest and the absence of routes for upward social mobility; and the increasing concentration of the poorest, the most disadvantaged, in a residualised rented housing sector.[31]

Carey Oppenheim and Lisa Harker, in the Child Poverty Action Group's *Poverty: The Facts*, likewise suggest that, despite their several objections to the use of the term, it arguably does help 'to capture an intensity of poverty. It conveys the ways in which different aspects of poverty such as low quality housing, a bleak urban environment, social isolation, exclusion from the world of paid work and lack of participation in political life compound one another'.[32]

Certainly, any report which purports to be about an 'underclass' rather than boring, old-fashioned, poverty is likely to receive greater media attention and thus it might be argued that use of the term, even by those who do not subscribe to Murray's thesis, is justified as a means of putting poverty in the headlines. However, as Murray declares, 'underclass is an ugly word' (p. 23). So too is the language of many who write about it. For instance, Murray describes himself as 'a visitor from a plague area come to see whether the disease is spreading' and he tells us that the question facing Britain is 'how contagious is this disease?' (p. 42). Similarly, Dahrendorf describes the 'underclass' as 'a cancer which eats away at the texture of societies' and its future development as 'critical for the moral hygiene of British society'.[33] The *Sunday Times*, in an editorial to mark its publication of Murray's first British essay commented that 'the underclass spawns illegitimate children', creating an image of breeding animals.[34] The label 'underclass', with all its negative connotations, now tends to be applied indiscriminately by the media to those in poverty.

The language of disease and contamination associated with the 'underclass' conveys a pathological image of people in poverty. This is nothing new. As John Macnicol has demonstrated, and as Murray himself notes, the 'underclass' label is simply the latest of many which have been stamped on that group of poor people perceived as undesirable and threatening.[35] As Mann observes 'one feature of the underclass which recurs in virtually every account, particularly the US literature, is the apprehension this class provokes in others. In many ways this class challenge the comfortable position of the middle classes at a time when the gap between the haves and have nots has widened'.[36]

I have argued elsewhere that those, like Dahrendorf and Field, who deploy the language of the 'underclass' in order to the make the case for the restoration of full citizenship rights to the poor 'are playing with fire'.[37] The danger is that the more that certain groups in poverty, or the poor generally, are described in the value-laden language of the 'underclass', the easier it becomes for the rest of society to write them off as beyond the bonds of common citizenship. The reaction is more likely to be defensive calls for tougher law and order policies than for an inclusive citizenship-based anti-poverty strategy. The use of stigmatising labels is likely to lead to stigmatising policies. Indeed, as Green makes clear in his original Foreword, the restoration of stigma as an instrument of social policy is part of the New Right's project.

Women who have children outside marriage are singled out as particularly worthy of stigma, the erosion of which since the 'sexual revolution of the 1960s', Murray suggests, has contributed to the increase in their numbers. This both reflects and has contributed to a general sharpening of the ideological debate around lone motherhood.[38] The gender agenda underlying Murray's preoccupation with single motherhood and marriage is highlighted in Sue Slipman's commentary where she points to his policy prescriptions which would force women on their own with children back into economic dependence on men. Thus Murray's essays contribute to the central goal of the IEA Health and Welfare Unit, identified by Green as the restoration of 'the ideal of the two parent family'.[39]

Blaming the 'Underclass'? Reconciling Structure and Agency

This explicit moralising agenda underlying Murray's account of the 'underclass' has prompted accusations, such as Alan Walker's in this volume, of 'blaming the victim'. Explanations of poverty which focus on the behaviour and values of those deemed to be members of the 'underclass' divert attention from wider social, economic and political causes. This, as Pete Alcock notes, has led many to prefer the less pejorative term of social exclusion. This is a more dynamic language which encourages a focus on the processes and institutions which create and maintain disadvantage rather than what can become a voyeuristic preoccupation with individual poor people and their behaviour. Social scientists are thereby encouraged no longer to gaze only in the direction of the poor and powerless, but also at the rest of society and, in particular, the powerful.[40] 'An "overclass", Mr Murray?' asks Walker. And indeed, Christopher Lasch has identified just such an overclass or élite who have excluded themselves from society and from the responsibilities of citizenship associated with membership of a society.[41] The concept of social polarisation, which would capture what is happening at the top as well as the bottom of society, has thus been advanced to complement that of social exclusion.[42]

This is how the battle lines have been drawn up between those who subscribe to structuralist and behaviouralist approaches in explaining poverty; what Robinson and Gregson refer to as the 'classic polarity' between structure and agency.[43] They, and some other commentators such as Smith, suggest that the notion of an 'under-class' might offer a way of breaking down this polarity in recognition of the possible interplay between structural and cultural or behavioural factors.

Certainly, we can observe in the literature about poverty a shift away from what could be interpreted as a structural determinism in which the poor are presented as simply powerless victims.[44] An emphasis on the structural constraints which limit the opportunities of disadvantaged groups needs to be balanced with a recognition that members of these groups are also agents or actors in their own lives. As actors there is ample evidence of the ways in which, both individually and collectively, people in poverty (and especially women) struggle to gain greater control over their own lives and to improve their situation and that of the communities in which they live. However, as actors they will make mistakes and 'wrong' decisions, like the rest of us, and there is a fine line between acknowledging the agency of people in poverty and blaming them for that poverty.

It is partly because the notion of an 'underclass' now carries such strong connotations of blame that I do not believe that it offers the means of reconciling structure and agency in helping us to understand poverty and thereby do something about it. Moreover, as I have argued, its imprecision renders it an unhelpful concept for shaping sociological research. The danger is that in searching for the 'underclass', social scientists, politicians and the media will fail to see on the one hand the structural forces which are pushing more and more people into poverty and on the other the resourcefulness and resilience with which many of these 'victims' respond.[45]

Notes

1   His two essays were published by the IEA: Murray, C., *The Emerging British Underclass*, London: IEA Health and Welfare Unit, 1990; and Murray, C., *Underclass: The Crisis Deepens*, London: IEA Health and Welfare Unit/Sunday Times, 1994.

2   I would like to thank Carey Oppenheim for her helpful comments on the first draft of this Introduction.

3   For a more detailed account of the history of the term 'underclass', see Robinson, F., and Gregson, R., 'The Underclass: A Class Apart?', *Critical Social Policy*, No. 34, 1992, pp. 38-51; Moore, R., 'Citizenship and the Underclass' in Coenen, H. and Leisink, P., *Work and Citizenship in the New Europe*, Aldershot: Edward Elgar, 1993; Mann, K., 'Watching the Defectives: Observers of the Underclass in the USA, Britain and Australia', *Critical Social Policy*, No. 41, 1994, pp.79-99; Morris, L., *Dangerous Classes: The Underclass and Social Citizenship*, London: Routledge, 1994.

4   Sivanandan, A., 'Le trahison des clercs', *New Statesman and Society*, 14 July 1995, pp. 20-21.

5   Moore, R., *op. cit.*, p. 60.

6   Dahrendorf, R., 'The Erosion of Citizenship and its Consequences for us all', *New Statesman*, 12 June 1987, p. 13.

7   Field, F., *Losing Out: the Emergence of Britain's Underclass*, Oxford: Blackwell, 1989, pp. 196 and 153.

8   See, for instance, Macnicol, J., 'In Pursuit of the Underclass', *Journal of Social Policy*, Vol. 16, No. 3, 1987, pp. 293-318; Alcock, P., *Understanding Poverty*, Basingstoke: Macmillan, 1993.

9   Jencks, C., 'What is the Underclass–and is it Growing?' *Focus*, Vol. 12, No. 1, 1989, p. 14.

10   Willetts, D., in Smith, D. (ed.), *Understanding the Underclass*, London: Policy Studies Institute, 1992, p. 48.

11   Runciman, W.R., 'How Many Classes are there in Contemporary British Society?', *Sociology*, Vol. 24, No. 3, 1990, p. 388.

12 For a critique of Runciman's definition on the grounds that it confuses institutional and market relations see, Dean, H. and Taylor-Gooby, P., *Dependency Culture*, Hemel Hempstead: Harvester Wheatsheaf, 1992.

13 Smith, D., *op. cit.*, p. 4. Pensioners are excluded on the grounds that their pension signifies a stable historic relationship to the labour market. The same applies to those living off capital who 'benefit from a historic relationship with the mode of production' *op. cit.*, p. 8.

14 Wilson, J., *The Truly Disadvantaged: The Inner City, the Underclass, and Public Policy*, Chicago: University of Chicago Press, 1987, p. 8.

15 Van Haitsma, M., 'A Contextual Definition of the Underclass' *Focus*, Vol. 12, No. 1. 1989, p. 28.

16 Prosser, W., 'The Underclass: Assessing What we have Learned', *Focus*, Vol. 13, No. 2, 1991, pp. 2 and 17.

17 Buck, N. in Smith, D. (ed.), *Understanding the Underclass*, London: Policy Studies Institute, 1992. p. 19.

18 Ford, R., Marsh, A. and McKay, S., *Changes in Lone Parenthood*, London: DSS/HMSO, 1995, p. 92.

19 Bradshaw, J. and Millar, J., *Lone Parent Families in the UK*, London: DSS/HMSO, 1991; Haskey, J., 'Estimated Numbers and Demographic Characteristics of One-parent Families in Great Britain', *Population Trends*, No. 65, 1991, pp. 35-47. It should be noted that this analysis is based on length of time since becoming a lone parent rather than completed spells of lone parenthood.

20 Ford, R., Marsh, A. and McKay, S., *Changes in Lone Parenthood*, London: DSS/HMSO, 1995, p. 92.

21 *Ibid.*

22 Ashworth, K., Walker, R. and Trinder, P., *Benefit Dynamics in Britain: Routes on and off Income Support*, Loughborough: Centre for Research in Social Policy, 1995, p. 31.

23 Webb, S., *Poverty Dynamics in Great Britain: Preliminary Analysis from the British Household Panel Survey*, London: Institute for Fiscal Studies, 1995, pp. 17-18.

24 Gallie, D., 'Are the Unemployed an Underclass? Some Evidence from the Social Change and Economic Life Initiative', *Sociology*, Vol. 28, No. 3, 1994, pp. 755-56.

25 Bradshaw, J. and Holmes, H., *Living on the Edge*, Tyneside: Child Poverty Action Group, 1989, p. 138.

26 Kempson, E., *Life on a Low Income*, York: Joseph Rowntree Foundation/York Publishing Services, 1996, p. 163.

27 Smith, D. (ed.), *Understanding the Underclass*, London: Policy Studies Institute, 1992, pp. 91 and 95.

28 For a discussion of the 'underclass' as discourse rather than objective phenomenon, see Dean, H. and Taylor-Gooby, P., *Dependency Culture*, Hemel Hempstead: Harvester Wheatsheaf, 1992.

29 Morris, L., *Dangerous Classes: The Underclass and Social Citizenship*, London: Routledge, 1994, p. 165.

30 Jencks, C., 'What is the Underclass–and is it Growing?', *Focus*, Vol. 12, No. 1, 1989, p. 25.

31 Robinson, F. and Gregson, R., 'The Underclass–A Class Apart?', *Critical Social Policy*, No. 34, 1992, p. 49.

32 Oppenheim, C. and Harker, L., *Poverty the Facts*, Third edition, London: Child Poverty Action Group, 1996, p. 17.

33 Dahrendorf, R., 'The Erosion of Citizenship and its Consequences for us all', *New Statesman*, June 1987, pp. 12 and 15.

34 The *Sunday Times*, 26 November 1989.

35 Macnicol, J., 'In Pursuit of the Underclass', *Journal of Social Policy*, Vol. 16, No. 3, 1987, pp. 293-318.

36 Mann, K., 'Watching the Defectives: Observers of the Underclass in the USA, Britain and Australia', *Critical Social Policy*, No. 41, 1994, p. 85.

37 Lister, R., *The Exclusive Society: Citizenship and the Poor*, London: Child Poverty Action Group, 1990, p. 26.

38 For a discussion in the British context see Lister, R., 'Back to the Family: Family Policies and Politics under the Major Government' in Jones, H. and Millar, J. (eds.), *The Politics of the Family*, Aldershot: Avebury, 1996.

39 Green, D.G., 'Foreword' to Dennis, N., *Rising Crime and the Dismembered Family*, London: IEA Health and Welfare Unit, 1993, p. viii; see also Davies, J. (ed.), *The Family: Is it Just Another Lifestyle Choice?*', London: IEA Health and Welfare Unit, 1993.

40 Mann, K., criticises those observers of the 'underclass' 'who gaze in only one direction; at the poor', *op. cit.*, p. 96.

41 Lasch, C., *The Revolt of the Elites and the Betrayal of Democracy*, London: W.W. Norton, 1995.

42 Scott, J., *Poverty and Wealth: Citizenship, Deprivation and Privilege*, Harlow: Longman, 1994; Williams, F. with Pillinger, J., 'New Thinking on Social Policy Research into Inequality, Social Exclusion and Poverty' in Millar, J. and Bradshaw, J. (eds.), *Social Welfare Systems: Towards a New Research Agenda*, Bath: Centre for Analysis of Social Policy in association with the Economic and Social Research Council, 1996.

43 Robinson and Gregson, *op. cit.*, 1992, p. 42.

44 See, for instance, Jordan, B., James, S., Kay, H., and Redley, M., *Trapped in Poverty?*, London: Routledge, 1992; Piachaud, D., *What's wrong with Fabianism?* London: Fabian Society, 1993; Williams, F. with Pillinger, J., *op. cit.*, 1996; Beresford, P., Green, D., Lister, R., and Woodward, K., *Poverty First Hand*, London: Child Poverty Action Group, forthcoming.

45 This resourcefulness and resilience is a theme running through Kempson's review of recent qualitative research into poverty, *op. cit.* 1996.

Part 1

The Emerging British Underclass

Foreword (1990 edition)

Charles Murray's *The Emerging British Underclass* was first published in the *Sunday Times Magazine* in November 1989 and we are now making it available in a more permanent form. The IEA's goal is to provide materials which can be used for teaching in schools, colleges, polytechnics and universities whilst also remaining accessible to the general reader and, to increase the value of Murray's paper as a teaching aid, it is being published with four commentaries by leading critics of his point of view. Charles Murray replies to their criticisms and develops his argument further in a Rejoinder.

Murray takes pains to explain that he does not apply the term underclass to all the poor, only to those distinguished by their undesirable behaviour, including drug-taking, crime, illegitimacy, failure to hold down a job, truancy from school and casual violence. He concentrates on three measures: crime, dropping out of the labour force and illegitimacy. He believes that illegitimacy is the best indicator of an underclass in the making and the rising trend of illegitimacy therefore alarms him. He contends that it is better that children should have two parents rather than one but believes there is a radical difference between different single-parent situations. Unlike divorce or widowhood, illegitimacy is a special problem, he says, because there is a single parent from day one and the child has not been the first consideration of the parents and may indeed be regarded as a mere encumbrance.

Crime too is growing and Murray cites with some amazement the statistic that there is more property crime in England and Wales than the US. His special concern, however, is crimes of violence particularly where whole neighbourhoods fall prey to criminality to such an extent that it becomes impossible for parents to raise their children to be unaggressive. No less alarming, Murray finds that a proportion of those who left school in the 1980s were not socialised into the world of work. He does not worry about this merely because other workers have to keep them at the public expense, but for their own sakes. Work is at the centre of life and without it, individuals are hard pressed to acquire and maintain both self-esteem and the respect of others. There is more to work than just making a living, says Murray.

Murray's assessment is that Britain has an underclass and that it is growing. He is frequently criticised for not offering a ready-made set of policies for governments to implement. The reason he refuses to prescribe alternative policies in detail is that, after spending much of his life implementing and appraising reform programmes, he has become pessimistic about the capacity of governments to engineer solutions at all. Providing jobs and training is not enough, he thinks, nor is tinkering with the benefit system sufficient. According to Murray, the only remedy is authentic self-government by local communities.

Murray's paper is published with four commentaries. Labour MP, Frank Field does not resist the use of the term underclass but defines it differently from Murray. In his view, it comprises three groups: the frail-elderly pensioner, single parents, and the long-term unemployed. Field's primary concern is to reduce inequalities of income and wealth, whilst the essence of Murray's approach is that a distinction should be made between low income as such and the behavioural poverty that results from conduct which is both anti-social and self-harming.

Joan Brown's paper challenges Murray's claim that single unmarried mothers constitute a special problem, pointing out that, according to a study by Ermisch, divorced mothers as a group spend longer on benefit than unwed mothers and that never-married mothers remain lone parents for a shorter average period than divorced mothers. Murray explains in his Rejoinder why he finds the Ermisch study wanting.

Alan Walker's essay is a forthright and unyielding statement of his socialist standpoint. He is an unrepentant egalitarian whose final assessment is that Murray's underclass theory 'blames the victim' and thus diverts our attention from blaming the mechanisms through which resources are distributed. Victim blaming is an attitude which Walker believes to have been at the root of many measures from the Elizabethan poor law to today's YTS and Restart programmes.

Professor Deakin's essay is dismissive and disdainful in tone, a tradition of social-policy writing popularised by Titmuss. His scorn for Murray leads him to conclude that Murray is advocating a kind of authoritarianism—a static form of society in which people are neatly docketed and from which the dangerous classes have been excluded, claims Deakin. This contention might without exaggeration be classified as audacious, since it is flatly contradicted by everything that Murray has ever said or written.

In his Rejoinder Murray offers a vigorous and good-humoured defence. He urges the necessity to conduct detailed sociological, one might say anthropological, studies in the field to bring investigators into face-to-face contact with the facts of human conduct; and he points to the dangers of relying too heavily on statistical interpretations which blur distinctions and conceal complexity by aggregation.

Finally, may I add a word of explanation for those who ask why classical liberals should be interested in these issues at all. What has individual freedom got to do with criticising the poor? The most important reason is that you cannot have a free society without morally-responsible citizens and you cannot have morally-responsible citizens unless we all take the trouble to tell each other when we are at fault and when we are doing well. People are fallible and we need the constant attention and support of others to keep us on the straight-and-narrow. That is why classical liberals mistrust political power. In Acton's oft-quoted words, 'Power tends to corrupt, and absolute power corrupts absolutely'. The classical-liberal remedy is government based on checks and balances and openness to criticism. Similarly, in economics human beings are fallible and may err on the side of selfishness. Classical liberals urge competition to check this tendency and direct possibly selfish energies into the service of others. Human beings are no less fallible in private life, and here it is the praise or blame of others mediated by conscience, or what Adam Smith called the impartial spectator, which guides us.

Yet in social policy it is considered inhumane to criticise or blame an individual who has fallen into hardship due to his own conduct. The humane approach is assumed to be to give money to the poor; anything else amounts to making excuses for not giving them money and is, accordingly, inhumane. But can it legitimately be claimed that to pass judgement on a person's conduct is automatically uncaring?

Consider the opposite of blame, praise. When we praise someone we applaud their achievement. We do so primarily to encourage still greater effort and achievement. Is blame not similar? We blame, we criticise, we judge, we censure in order to encourage people to do better next time. For years the *bête noire* of the social-policy mainstream has been stigma, which originally meant a mark branded on a slave or criminal. Social policies have been designed and redesigned in the hope of avoiding stigma. And to avoid stigmatising someone appears at first sight to be humane because it would be wholly wrong to brand someone a failure, or to stain their character permanently. But if we criticise a person who has fallen on hard times due to their own inappropriate behaviour, we do not brand them failures in some absolute or permanent sense. We spend our time criticising them because we believe them capable of more.

Failure never hurt anyone because it is through our failures as well as our successes that we grow. To criticise a person is to treat them as a dignified individual capable of functioning as a morally-responsible citizen. To refrain from criticising individuals whose conduct may be self-injuring as well as harmful to others, is in a fundamental sense to write them off as not worth bothering with. It is to treat them as the powerless victims of circumstance and thus to fail to acknowledge the very capacity that makes us all human, our ability to act as thinking, valuing, choosing individuals.

We can learn something from our forbears about combining humanity with praise and blame. It might well be callous to refuse to help someone on the ground that they were the author of their own misfortune. People should be helped whether or not they are to blame, wholly or partly for their own predicament. The important question is *how* they should be helped. In the days when self-help was the norm and the majority joined mutual aid societies to make provision against hard times, callous disregard for the unfortunate was denounced. The Manchester Unity friendly society, a million-strong voluntary association of workers for mutual aid and one of many similar organisations the membership of which far outnumbered that of the trade unions until the Second World War, enjoined its members to combine caring with criticism:

> In extending our charity we must endeavour to distinguish the really deserving, for those who willingly and professionally seek the charity of others forfeit all self-respect, and, in being content so to live, sacrifice personal dignity.

The duty of the Manchester Unity member in such cases was to try to awaken the 'love of independence'. But, this was not a policy of callous disregard:

> those who unworthily seek assistance are not to be neglected if really in distress; the voice of misery, proceed from whence it may, should never be disregarded. However, after relieving the actual wants of these unhappy persons, we should endeavour to raise them from the degradation into which they have fallen, and make them richer in their own esteem. As it is better that ten guilty persons escape than that one innocent should suffer, so it is better that ten undeserving persons be assisted than that one worthy be neglected.

To refrain from judging people is to refrain from respecting them. Perhaps it is time for social policy analysts to adopt a new rallying cry: Bring back stigma; all is forgiven!

David G. Green

The Emerging British Underclass

Charles Murray

The Concept of 'Underclass'

'Underclass' is an ugly word, with its whiff of Marx and the lumpenproletariat. Perhaps because it is ugly, 'underclass' as used in Britain tends to be sanitised, a sort of synonym for people who are not just poor, but especially poor. So let us get it straight from the outset: the 'underclass' does not refer to degree of poverty, but to a type of poverty.

It is not a new concept. I grew up knowing what the underclass was; we just didn't call it that in those days. In the small Iowa town where I lived, I was taught by my middle-class parents that there were two kinds of poor people. One class of poor people was never even called 'poor'. I came to understand that they simply lived with low incomes, as my own parents had done when they were young. Then there was another set of poor people, just a handful of them. These poor people didn't lack just money. They were defined by their behaviour. Their homes were littered and unkempt. The men in the family were unable to hold a job for more than a few weeks at a time. Drunkenness was common. The children grew up ill-schooled and ill-behaved and contributed a disproportionate share of the local juvenile delinquents.

British observers of the nineteenth century knew these people. To Henry Mayhew, whose articles in the *Morning Chronicle* in 1850 drew the Victorians' attention to poverty, they were the 'dishonest poor', a member of which was:

> distinguished from the civilised man by his repugnance to regular and continuous labour—by his want of providence in laying up a store for the future—by his inability to perceive consequences ever so slightly removed from immediate apprehensions—by his passion for stupefying herbs and roots and, when possible, for intoxicating fermented liquors...

Other popular labels were 'undeserving', 'unrespectable', 'depraved', 'debased', 'disreputable' or 'feckless' poor.

As Britain entered the 1960s a century later, this distinction between honest and dishonest poor people had been softened. The second kind of poor person was no longer 'undeserving'; rather, he was the product of a 'culture of poverty'. But intellectuals as well as the man in the street continued to accept that poor people were not all alike. Most were doing their best under difficult circumstances; a small number were pretty much as Mayhew had described them. Then came the intellectual reformation that swept both the United States and Britain at about the same time, in the mid-1960s, and with it came a new way of looking at the poor. Henceforth, the poor were to be homogenised. The only difference between poor people and everyone else, we were told, was that the poor had less money. More importantly, the poor were all alike. There was not such thing as the ne'er-do-well poor person—he was the figment of the prejudices of a parochial middle class. Poor people, *all* poor people, were equally victims, and would be equally successful if only society gave them a fair shake.

The Difference between the US and the UK

The difference between the United States and Britain was that the United States reached the future first. During the last half of the 1960s and throughout the 1970s something strange and frightening was happening among poor people in the United States. Poor communities that had consisted mostly of hardworking folks began deteriorating, sometimes falling apart altogether. Drugs, crime, illegitimacy, homelessness, drop-out from the job market, drop-out from school, casual violence—all the measures that were available to the social scientists showed large increases, focused in poor communities. As the 1980s began, the growing population of 'the other kind of poor people' could no longer be ignored, and a label for them came into use. In the US, we began to call them the underclass.

For a time, the intellectual conventional wisdom continued to hold that underclass was just another pejorative attempt to label the poor. But the label had come into use because there was no longer any denying reality. What had once been a small fraction of the American poor had become a sizeable and worrisome population. An underclass existed, and none of the ordinary kinds of social policy solutions seemed able to stop its growth. One by one, the American social scientists who had initially rejected the concept of an underclass fell silent, then began to use it themselves.

By and large, British intellectuals still disdain the term. In 1987, the social historian John Macnicol summed up the prevailing view in the *Journal of Social Policy,* writing dismissively that underclass was nothing more than a refuted concept periodically resurrected by Conservatives 'who wish to constrain the redistributive potential of state welfare'.[1] But there are beginning to be breaks in the ranks. Frank Field, the prominent Labour MP, has just published a book with 'underclass' in its subtitle. The newspapers, watching the United States and seeing shadows of its problems in Britain, have begun to use the term. As someone who has been analysing this phenomenon in the United States, I arrived in Britain earlier this year, a visitor from a plague area come to see whether the disease is spreading.

With all the reservations that a stranger must feel in passing judgement on an unfamiliar country, I will jump directly to the conclusion: Britain does have an underclass, still largely out of sight and still smaller than the one in the United States. But it is growing rapidly. Within the next decade, it will probably become as large (proportionately) as the United States' underclass. It could easily become larger.

I am not talking here about an unemployment problem that can be solved by more jobs, nor about a poverty problem that can be solved by higher benefits. Britain has a growing population of working-aged, healthy people who live in a different world from other Britons, who are raising their children to live in it, and whose values are now contaminating the life of entire neighbourhoods—which is one of the most insidious aspects of the phenomenon, for neighbours who don't share those values cannot isolate themselves.

There are many ways to identify an underclass. I will concentrate on three phenomena that have turned out to be early warning signals in the United States: illegitimacy, violent crime, and drop-out from the labour force. In each case I will be using the simplest of data, collected and published by Britain's Government Statistical Service. I begin with illegitimacy, which in my view is the best predictor of an underclass in the making.

Illegitimacy and the Underclass

It is a proposition that angers many people. Why should it be a 'problem' that a woman has a child without a husband? Why isn't a single woman perfectly capable of raising a healthy, happy child, if only the state will provide a decent level of support so that she may do so? Why is raising a child without having married any more of a problem than raising a child after a divorce? The very world 'illegitimate' is intellectually illegitimate. Using it in a gathering of academics these days is a *faux pas,* causing pained silence.

I nonetheless focus on illegitimacy rather than on the more general phenomenon of one-parent families because, in a world where all social trends are ambiguous, illegitimacy is less ambiguous than other forms of single parenthood. It is a matter of degree. Of course some unmarried mothers are excellent mothers and some unmarried fathers are excellent fathers. Of course some divorced parents disappear from the children's lives altogether and some divorces have more destructive effects on the children than a failure to marry would have had. Being without two parents is generally worse for the child than having two parents, no matter how it happens. But illegitimacy is the purest form of being without two parents—legally, the child is without a father from day one; he is often without one practically as well. Further, illegitimacy bespeaks an attitude on the part of one or both parents that getting married is not an essential part of siring or giving birth to a child; this in itself distinguishes their mindset from that of people who do feel strongly that getting married is essential.

Call it what you will, illegitimacy has been sky-rocketing since 1979. I use 'sky-rocketing' advisedly. In Figure 1 (p. 53) for the years since the Second World War ended, the post-war era divides into three parts. From the end of the Second World War until 1960, Britain enjoyed a very low and even slightly declining illegitimacy ratio. From 1960 until 1978 the ratio increased, but remained modest by international standards—as late as 1979, Britain's illegitimacy ratio was only 10.6 per cent, one of the lowest rates in the industrialised West. Then, suddenly, during a period when fertility was steady, the illegitimacy ratio began to rise very rapidly—to 14.1 per cent by 1982, 18.9 per cent by 1985, and finally to 25.6 per cent by 1988. If present trends continue, Britain will pass the United States in this unhappy statistic in 1990.

The sharp rise is only half of the story. The other and equally important half is that illegitimate births are not scattered evenly among the British population. In this, press reports can be misleading. There is much publicity about the member of the royal family who has a child without a husband, or the socially prominent young career woman who deliberately decides to have a baby on her own, but these are comparatively rare events. The increase in illegitimate births is strikingly concentrated among the lowest social class.

Municipal Districts

This is especially easy to document in Britain, where one may fit together the Government Statistical Service's birth data on municipal districts with the detailed socio-economic data from the general census. When one does so for 169 metropolitan districts and boroughs in England and Wales with data from both sources, the relationship between social class and illegitimacy is so obvious that the statistical tests become superfluous. Municipal districts with high concentrations of household heads in Class I (professional persons, by the classification used for many years by the Government Statistical Service) have illegitimacy ratios in the low teens (Wokingham was lowest as of 1987, with only nine of every 100 children born illegitimate) while municipalities like Nottingham and Southwark, with populations most heavily weighed with Class V household heads (unskilled labourers), have illegitimacy ratios of more than 40 per cent (the highest in 1987 was Lambeth, with 46 per cent).

The statistical tests confirm this relationship. The larger the proportion of people who work at unskilled jobs and the larger the proportion who are out of the labour force, the higher the illegitimacy ratio, in a quite specific and regular numeric relationship. The strength of the relationship may be illustrated this way: suppose you were limited to two items of information about a community—the percentage of people in Class V and the percentage of people who are 'economically inactive'. With just these two measures, you could predict the illegitimacy ratio, usually within just three percentage points of the true number. As a statistician might summarise it, these two measures of economic status 'explain 51 per cent of the variance'—an extremely strong relationship by the standards of the social sciences.

It short, the notion that illegitimate births are a general phenomenon, that young career women and girls from middle-class homes are doing it just as much as anyone else, is flatly at odds with the facts. There has been a *proportional* increase in illegitimate births among all communities, but the *prevalence* of illegitimate births is drastically higher among the lower-class communities than among the upper-class ones.

Neighbourhoods

The data I have just described are based on municipal districts. The picture gets worse when we move down to the level of the neighbourhood, though precise numbers are hard to come by. The proportion of illegitimate children in a specific poor neighbourhood can be in the vicinity not of 25 per cent, nor even of 40 per cent, but a hefty majority. And in this concentration of illegitimate births lies a generational catastrophe. Illegitimacy produces an underclass for one compelling practical reason having nothing to do with morality or the sanctity of marriage. Namely: communities need families. Communities need fathers.

This is not an argument that many intellectuals in Britain are ready to accept. I found that discussing the issue was like being in a time warp, hearing in 1989 the same rationalisations about illegitimacy that American experts used in the 1970s and early 1980s.

'Children from Single-parent Households do just as well as Children from Two-parent Households'

For example, there is the case of the National Child Development Study (NCDS), a longitudinal sample that researchers have been following since 1968. The differences between children from one-parent families and two-parent families are due to social and financial circumstances, not to the parental situation, proclaims a set of studies in *Growing Up in Great Britain,* prepared under the auspices of the National Children's Bureau.

Assessing these conclusions is made difficult by technical problems with the way that 'single-parent' and 'two-parent' families were defined (for example, a child could be defined as coming from a one-parent family if he had ever been without two parents, even briefly). But the generic problem with such analyses, and these in particular, is that all forms of single parenthood tend to be lumped together, as if it makes no difference whether the mother is a widow, a middle-aged woman divorced after years of marriage, or a girl of 20 who has never married. All are 'single parents', and all single-parent situations are equal. I am asserting something very different: one particular form of single-parenthood—illegitimacy—constitutes a special problem for society. Single-parent situations are radically unequal.

The change in the received wisdom on this topic in the US has been remarkable. One example will serve to illustrate. In 1983, a statistic cited everywhere by those who would debunk the reactionaries was that 50 per cent of all US welfare mothers were off the welfare rolls within two years. The idea of 'welfare dependency' was a myth. Then, in 1986, David Ellwood, the scholar whose work had popularised the 50 per cent statistic, took a closer look at the same data (a large longitudinal study), separating welfare mothers into different categories. It turned out that one factor made a huge difference how quickly a woman left welfare: whether she had been married. The short-term welfare recipients were concentrated among those who had found themselves on welfare after a divorce. For the never-married woman, the average number of years on welfare was not the highly touted 2 years, but 9.3. What the people who live in Harlem and the South Bronx had known for years was finally discovered by social science: long-term welfare dependency is a fact, not a myth, among young women who have children without husbands. A similar shift in the received wisdom is occurring in research on delinquency, education, emotional development and health. Just as the scholarly mainstream has had to confront the reality of an underclass, researchers are asking new and better questions of the data about marital status, and getting more accurate answers. Even after economic circumstances are matched, the children of single mothers do worse, often much worse, than the children of married couples.

'Mainly a Black Problem'?

'It's mainly a black problem'. I heard this everywhere, from political clubs in Westminster to some quite sophisticated demographers in the statistical research offices. The statement is correct in this one, very limited sense: blacks born in the West Indies have much higher illegitimacy ratios—about 48 per cent of live births in the latest numbers—than all whites. But blacks constitute such a tiny proportion of the British population that their contribution to the overall illegitimacy ratio is minuscule. If there had been no blacks whatsoever in Britain (and I am including all blacks in Britain in this statement, not just those who were born abroad), the overall British illegitimacy ratio in 1988 would have dropped by about one percentage point, from 25 per cent to about 24 per cent. Blacks are not causing Britain's illegitimacy problem.

In passing, it is worth adding that the overall effect of ethnic minorities living in the UK is to *reduce* the size of the illegitimacy ratio. The Chinese, Indians, Pakistanis, Arabs and East Africans in Britain have illegitimacy ratios that are tiny compared with those of British whites.

'It's Not as Bad as it Looks'

In the United States, the line used to be that blacks have extended families, with uncles and grandfathers compensating for the lack of a father. In Britain, the counterpart to this cheery optimism is that an increasing number of illegitimate births are jointly registered and that an increasing number of such children are born to people who live together at the time of birth. Both joint registration and living together are quickly called evidence of 'a stable relationship'.

The statements about joint registration and living together are factually correct. Of the 158,500 illegitimate births in England and Wales in 1987, 69 per cent were jointly registered. Of those who jointly registered the birth, 70 per cent gave the same address, suggesting some kind of continuing relationship. Both of these figures have increased—in 1961, for example' only 38 per cent of illegitimate births were jointly registered, suggesting that the nature of illegitimacy in the United Kingdom has changed dramatically.

You may make what you wish of such figures. In the United States, we have stopped talking blithely about the 'extended family' in black culture that would make everything okay. It hasn't. And as the years go on, the extended family argument becomes a cruel joke—for without marriage, grandfathers and uncles too become scarce. In Britain, is it justified to assume that jointly registering a birth, or living together at the time of the birth, means a relationship that is just as stable (or nearly as stable) as a marriage? I pose it as a question because I don't have the empirical answer. But neither did any of the people who kept repeating the joint-registration and living-together numbers so optimistically.

If we can be reasonably confident that the children of never married women do considerably worse than their peers, it remains to explain why. Progress has been slow. Until recently in the United States, scholars were reluctant to concede that illegitimacy is a legitimate variable for study. Even as that situation changes, they remain slow to leave behind their equations and go out to talk with people who are trying to raise their children in neighbourhoods with high illegitimacy rates. This is how I make sense of the combination of quantitative studies, ethnographic studies and talking-to-folks journalism that bear on the question of illegitimacy, pulling in a few observations from my conversations in Britain

Clichés about Role Models are True

It turns out that the cliches about role models are true. Children grow up making sense of the world around them in terms of their own experience. Little boys don't naturally grow up to be responsible fathers and husbands. They don't naturally grow up knowing how to get up every morning at the same time and go to work. They don't naturally grow up thinking that work is not just a way to make money, but a way to hold one's head high in the world. And most emphatically of all, little boys do not reach adolescence naturally wanting to refrain from sex, just as little girls don't become adolescents naturally wanting to refrain from having babies. In all these ways and many more, boys and girls grow into responsible parents and neighbours and workers because they are imitating the adults around them.

That's why single-parenthood is a problem for communities, and that's why illegitimacy is the most worrisome aspect of single-parenthood. Children tend to behave like the adults around them. A child with a mother and no father, living in a neighbourhood of mothers with no fathers, judges by what he sees. You can send in social workers and school teachers and clergy to tell a young male that when he grows up he should be a good father to his children, but he doesn't know what that means unless he's seen it. Fifteen years ago, there was hardly a poor neighbourhood in urban Britain where children did not still see plentiful examples of good fathers around them. Today, the balance has already shifted in many poor neighbourhoods. In a few years, the situation will be much worse, for this is a problem that nurtures itself.

Child-Rearing in Single-Parent Communities

Hardly any of this gets into the public dialogue. In the standard newspaper or television story on single-parenthood, the reporter tracks down a struggling single parent and reports her efforts to raise her children under difficult circumstances, ending with an indictment of a stingy social system that doesn't give her enough to get along.

The ignored story is what it's like for the two-parent families trying to raise their children in neighbourhoods where they now represent the exception, not the rule. Some of the problems may seem trivial but must be painfully poignant to anyone who is a parent. Take, for example, the story told me by a father who lives in such a neighbourhood in Birkenhead, near Liverpool, about the time he went to his little girl's Christmas play at school. He was the only father there—hardly any of the other children had fathers—and his daughter, embarrassed because she was different, asked him not to come to the school anymore.

The lack of fathers is also associated with a level of physical unruliness that makes life difficult. The same Birkenhead father and his wife raised their first daughter as they were raised, to be polite and considerate—and she suffered for it. Put simply, her schoolmates weren't being raised to be polite and considerate —they weren't being 'raised' at all in some respects. We have only a small body of systematic research on child-rearing practices in contemporary low-income, single-parent communities; it's one of those unfashionable topics. But the unsystematic reports I heard in towns like Birkenhead and council estates like Easterhouse in Glasgow are consistent with the reports from inner-city Washington and New York: in communities without fathers, the kids tend to run wild. The fewer the fathers, the greater the tendency. 'Run wild' can mean such simple things as young children having no set bedtime. It can mean their being left alone in the house at night while mummy goes out. It can mean an 18-month-old toddler allowed to play in the street. And, as in the case of the couple trying to raise their children as they had been raised, it can mean children who are inordinately physical and aggressive in their relationships with other children. With their second child, the Birkenhead parents eased up on their requirements for civil behaviour, realising that their children had to be able to defend themselves against threats that the parents hadn't faced when they were children. The third child is still an infant, and the mother has made a conscious decision. 'I won't knock the aggression out of her,' she said to me. Then she paused, and added angrily, 'It's *wrong* to have to decide that.'

The Key to an Underclass

I can hear the howls of objection already—lots of families raise children who have those kinds of problems, not just poor single parents. Of course. But this is why it is important to talk to parents who have lived in both kinds of communities. Ask them whether there is any difference in child-raising between a neighbourhood composed mostly of married couples and a neighbourhood composed mostly of single mothers. In Britain as in the United States—conduct the inquiries yourself—the overwhelming response is that the difference is large and palpable. The key to an underclass is not the individual instance but a situation in which a very large proportion of an entire community lacks fathers, and this is far more common in poor communities than in rich ones.

Crime and the Underclass

Crime is the next place to look for an underclass, for several reasons. First and most obviously, the habitual criminal is the classic member of an underclass. He lives off mainstream society without participating in it. But habitual criminals are only part of the problem. Once again, the key issue in thinking about an underclass is how the community functions, and crime can devastate a community in two especially important ways. To the extent that the members of a community are victimised by crime, the community tends to become fragmented. To the extent that many people in a community engage in crime as a matter of course, all sorts of the socialising norms of the community change, from the kind of men that the younger boys choose as heroes to the standards of morality in general.

Consider first the official crime figures, reported annually for England by the Home Office. As in the case of illegitimacy, I took for granted before I began this exploration that England had much lower crime rates than the United States. It therefore came as a shock to discover that England and Wales (which I will subsequently refer to as England) have a combined property crime rate apparently as high, and probably higher, than that of the United States. (I did not compare rates with Scotland and Northern Ireland, which are reported separately.) I say 'apparently' because Britain and the United States use somewhat different definitions of property crime. But burglaries, which are similarly defined in both countries, provide an example. In 1988, England had 1,623 reported burglaries per 100,000 population compared with 1,309 in the US. Adjusting for the transatlantic differences in definitions, England also appears to have had higher rates of motor vehicle theft than the United States. The rates for other kind of theft seem to have been roughly the same. I wasn't the only one who was surprised at these comparisons. I found that if you want to attract startled and incredulous attention in England, mention casually that England has a higher property crime rate than that notorious crime centre of the western world, the United States. No one will believe you.

Violent Crime

The understandable reason why they don't believe you is that *violent* crime in England remains much lower than violent crime in the United States, and it is violent crime that engenders most anxiety and anger. In this regard, Britain still lags far behind the US. This is most conspicuously true for the most violent of all crimes, homicide. In all of 1988, England and Wales recorded just 624 homicides. The United States averaged that many every 11 days—20,675 for the year.

That's the good news. The bad news is that the violent crime rate in England and Wales has been rising very rapidly, as shown in Figure 2 (p. 53).

The size of the increase isn't as bad as it first looks, because England began with such a small initial rate (it's easy to double your money if you start with only a few pence—of which, more in a moment). Still, the rise is steep, and it became much steeper in about 1968. Compare the gradual increase from 1955 to 1968 with what happened subsequently. By 1988, England had 314 violent crimes reported per 100,000 people. The really bad news is that you have been experiencing this increase despite demographic trends that should have been working to your advantage. This point is important enough to explain at greater length.

The most frequent offenders, the ones who puff up the violent crime statistics, are males in the second half of their teens. As males get older, they tend to become more civilised. In both England and the United States, the number of males in this troublesome age group increased throughout the 1970s, and this fact was widely used as an explanation for increasing crime. But since the early 1980s, the size of the young male cohort has been decreasing in both countries. In the United Kingdom, for example, the number of males aged 15 to 19 hit its peak in 1982 and has subsequently decreased both as a percentage of the population and in raw numbers (by a little more than 11 per cent in both cases). Ergo, the violent crime rate 'should' have decreased as well. But it didn't. Despite the reduction in the number of males in the highest-offending age group after 1982, the violent crime rate in England from 1982 to 1988 rose by 43 per cent.

Here I must stop and briefly acknowledge a few of the many ways in which people will object that the official crime rates don't mean anything—but only briefly, because this way lies a statistical abyss.

The Significance of Official Crime Rates

One common objection is that the increase in the crime rate reflects economic growth (because there are more things to steal, especially cars and the things in them) rather than any real change in criminal behaviour. If so, one has to ask why England enjoyed a steady decline in crime through the last half of the 19th century, when economic growth was explosive. But, to avoid argument, let us acknowledge that economic growth does make interpreting the changes in the property crime rate tricky, and focus instead on violent crime, which is not so directly facilitated by economic growth.

Another common objection is that the increase in crime is a mirage. One version of this is that crime just seems to be higher because more crimes are being reported to the police than before (because of greater access to telephones, for example, or because of the greater prevalence of insurance). The brief answer here is that it works both ways. Rape and sexual assault are more likely to be reported now, because of changes in public attitudes and judicial procedures regarding those crimes. An anonymous purse-snatch is less likely to be reported, because the victim doesn't think it will do any good. The aggregate effect of a high crime rate can be to reduce reporting, and this is most true of poor neighbourhoods where attitudes toward the police are ambiguous.

The most outrageously spurious version of the 'crime isn't really getting worse' argument uses *rate* of increase rather than the *magnitude* of increase to make the case. The best example in Britain is the argument that public concern about muggings in the early 1970s was simply an effort to scapegoat young blacks, and resulted in a 'moral panic'. The sociologist Stuart Hall and his colleagues made this case at some length in a book entitled *Policing the Crisis*,[2] in which, among other things, they blithely argued that because the rate of increase in violent crimes was decreasing, the public's concern was unwarranted. It is the familiar problem of low baselines. From 1950 to 1958, violent crime in England rose by 88 per cent (the crime rate began at 14 crimes per 100,000 persons and rose by 13). From 1980 to 1988, violent crime in England rose by only 60 per cent (it began at 196 crimes per 100,000 persons and rose by 118). In other words, by the logic of Hall and his colleagues, things are getting much better, because the rate of increase in the 1980s has been lower than it was during the comparable period of the 1950s. Now take another look at the graph of violent crime. Is everyone convinced?

The Intellectual Conventional Wisdom

The denial by intellectuals that crime really has been getting worse spills over into denial that poor communities are more violent places than affluent communities. To the people who live in poor communities, this doesn't make much sense. One man in a poor, high-crime community told me about his experience in an open university where he had decided to try to improve himself. He took a sociology course about poverty. The professor kept talking about this 'nice little world that the poor live in', the man remembered. The professor scoffed at the reactionary myth that poor communities are violent places. To the man who lived in such a community, it was 'bloody drivel'. A few weeks later, a class exercise called for the students to canvass a poor neighbourhood. The professor went along, but apparently he, too, suspected that some of this pronouncements were bloody drivel— he cautiously stayed in his car and declined to knock on doors himself. And that raises the most interesting question regarding the view that crime has not risen, or that crime is not especially a problem in lower-class communities: do any of the people who hold this view actually *believe* it, to the extent that they take no more precautions walking in a slum neighbourhood than they do in a middle-class suburb?

These comments will not still the battle over the numbers. But I will venture this prediction, once again drawn from the American experience. After a few more years, quietly and without anyone having to admit he had been wrong, the intellectual conventional wisdom in Britain as in the United States will undergo a gradual transition. After all the statistical artifacts are taken into account and argued over, it will be decided that England is indeed becoming a more dangerous place in which to live: that this unhappy process is not occurring everywhere, but disproportionately in particular types of neighbourhoods; and that those neighbourhoods turn out to be the ones in which an underclass is taking over. Reality will once again force theory to its knees.

Unemployment and the Underclass

If illegitimate births are the leading indicator of an underclass and violent crime a proxy measure of its development, the definitive proof that an underclass has arrived is that large numbers of young, healthy, low-income males choose not to take jobs. (The young idle rich are a separate problem.) This decrease in labour force participation is the most elusive of the trends in the growth of the British underclass.

The main barrier to understanding what's going on is the high unemployment of the 1980s. The official statistics distinguish between 'unemployed' and 'economically inactive', but Britain's unemployment figures (like those in the US) include an unknown but probably considerable number of people who manage to qualify for benefit even if in reality very few job opportunities would tempt them to work.

On the other side of the ledger, over a prolonged period of high unemployment the 'economically inactive' category includes men who would like to work but have given up. To make matters still more complicated, there is the 'black economy' to consider, in which people who are listed as 'economically inactive' are really working for cash, not reporting their income to the authorities. So we are looking through a glass darkly, and I have more questions than answers.

Economic Inactivity and Social Class

The simple relationship of economic inactivity to social class is strong, just as it was for illegitimacy. According to the 1981 census data, the municipal districts with high proportions of household heads who are in Class V (unskilled labour) also tend to have the highest levels of 'economically inactive' persons of working age (statistically, the proportion of Class V households explains more than a third of the variance when inactivity because of retirement is taken into account).

This is another way of saying that you will find many more working-aged people who are neither working nor looking for work in the slums than in the suburbs. Some of these persons are undoubtedly discouraged workers, but two questions need to be asked and answered with far more data than are currently available—specifically, questions about lower-class young males.

Lower-Class Young Males

First, after taking into account Britain's unemployment problems when the 1981 census was taken, were the levels of economic inactivity among young males consistent with the behaviour of their older brothers and fathers during earlier periods? Or were they dropping out more quickly and often than earlier cohorts of young men?

Second, Britain has for the past few years been conducting a natural experiment, with an economic boom in the south and high unemployment in the north. If lack of jobs is the problem, then presumably economic inactivity among lower-class healthy young males in the south has plummeted to insignificant levels. Has it?

The theme that I heard from a variety of people in Birkenhead and Easterhouse was that the youths who came of age in the late 1970s are in danger of being a lost generation. All of them did indeed ascribe the problem to the surge in unemployment at the end of the 1970s. 'They came out of school at the wrong time,' as one older resident of Easterhouse put it, and have never in their lives held a real job. They are now in their late twenties. As economic times improve, they are competing for the same entry-level jobs as people 10 years younger, and employers prefer to hire the youngsters. But it's more complicated than that, he added. 'They've lost the picture of what they're going to be doing.' When he was growing up, he could see himself in his father's job. Not these young men.

The Generation Gap

This generation gap was portrayed to me as being only a few years wide. A man from Birkenhead in his early thirties who had worked steadily from the time he left school until 1979, when he lost his job as an assembly-line worker, recalled how the humiliation and desperation to work remained even as his unemployment stretched from months into years. He—and the others in their thirties and forties and fifties—were the ones showing up at six in the morning when jobs were advertised. They were the ones who sought jobs even if they paid less than the benefit rate.

'The only income I wanted was enough to be free of the bloody benefit system,' he said. 'It was like a rope around my neck.' The phrase for being on benefit that some of them used, 'on the suck', says a great deal about how little they like their situation.

This attitude is no small asset to Britain. In some inner cities of the US, the slang for robbing someone is 'getting paid'. Compare that inversion of values with the values implied by 'on the suck'. Britain in 1989 has resources that make predicting the course of the underclass on the basis of the US experience very dicey.

But the same men who talk this way often have little in common with their sons and younger brothers. Talking to the boys in their late teens and early twenties about jobs, I heard nothing about the importance of work as a source of self-respect and no talk of just wanting enough income to be free of the benefit system. To make a decent living, a youth of 21 explained to me, you need £200 a week—after taxes. He would accept less if it was all he could get. But he conveyed clearly that he would feel exploited. As for the Government's employment training scheme, YTS, that's 'slave labour'. Why, another young man asked me indignantly, should he and his friends be deprived of their right to a full unemployment benefit just because they haven't reached 18 yet? It sounded strange to my ears—a 'right' to unemployment benefit for a school-age minor who's never held a job. But there is no question in any of their minds that that's exactly what the unemployment benefit is: a right, in every sense of the word. The boys did not mention what they considered to be their part of the bargain.

'I was brought up thinking work is something you are morally obliged to do,' as one older man put it. With the younger generation, he said, 'that culture isn't going to be there at all.' And there are anecdotes to go with these observations. For example, the contractors carrying out the extensive housing refurbishment now going on at Easterhouse are obliged to hire local youths for unskilled labour as part of a work-experience scheme. Thirty Easterhouse young men applied for a recent set of openings. Thirteen were accepted. Ten actually came to work the first day. By the end of the first week, only one was still showing up.

A Generation Gap by Class

My hypothesis—the evidence is too fragmentary to call it more than that—is that Britain is experiencing a generation gap by class. Well-educated young people from affluent homes are working in larger proportions and working longer hours than ever. The attitudes and behaviour of the middle-aged working class haven't changed much. The change in stance toward the labour force is concentrated among lower-class young men in their teens and twenties. It is not a huge change. I am not suggesting that a third or a quarter or even a fifth of lower-class young people are indifferent to work. An underclass doesn't have to be huge to become a problem.

That problem is remarkably difficult to fix. It seems simple— just make decent-paying jobs available. But it doesn't work that way. In the States, we've tried nearly everything— training programmes, guaranteed jobs, special 'socialisation' programmes that taught not only job skills but also 'work-readiness skills' such as getting to work on time, 'buddy' systems whereby an experienced older man tried to ease the trainee into the world of work. The results of these strategies, carefully evaluated against control groups, have consistently showed little effect at best, no effect most commonly, and occasionally negative effects.

If this seems too pessimistic for British youth, the Government or some private foundation may easily try this experiment: go down to the Bull Ring near Waterloo Bridge where one of London's largest cardboard cities is located. Pass over the young men who are alcoholics or drug addicts or mentally disturbed, selecting only those who seem clear-headed (there are many). Then offer them jobs at a generous wage for unskilled labour and see what happens. Add in a training component if you wish. Or, if you sympathise with their lack of interest in unskilled jobs, offer them more extensive training that would qualify them for skilled jobs. Carry out your promises to them, spend as much as you wish, and measure the results after 2 years against the experience of similar youths who received no such help. I am betting that you, too, will find 'no effect'. It is an irretrievable disaster for young men to grow up without being socialised into the world of work.

Work is at the Centre of Life

The reason why it is a disaster is not that these young men cause upright taxpayers to spend too much money supporting them. That is a nuisance. The disaster is to the young men themselves and the communities in which they live. Looking around the inner cities of the United States, a view which has been eloquently voiced in the past by people as disparate as Thomas Carlyle and Karl Marx seems increasingly validated by events: work is at the centre of life. By remaining out of the work force during the crucial formative years, young men aren't just losing a few years of job experience. They are missing out on the time in which they need to have been acquiring the skills and the networks of friends and experiences that enable them to establish a place for themselves— not only in the workplace, but a vantage point from which they can make sense of themselves and their lives.

Furthermore, when large numbers of young men don't work, the communities around them break down, just as they break down when large numbers of young unmarried women have babies. The two phenomena are intimately related. Just as work is more important than merely making a living, getting married and raising a family are more than a way to pass the time. Supporting a family is a central means for a man to prove to himself that he is a 'mensch'. Men who do not support families find other ways to prove that they are men, which tend to take various destructive forms. As many have commented through the centuries, young males are essentially barbarians for whom marriage—meaning not just the wedding vows, but the act of taking responsibility for a wife and children—is an indispensable civilising force. Young men who don't work don't make good marriage material. Often they don't get married at all; when they do, they haven't the ability to fill their traditional role. In either case, too many of them remain barbarians.

The Size of the British Underclass

How big is the British underclass? It all depends on how one defines its membership; trying to take a headcount is a waste of time. The size of the underclass can be made to look huge or insignificant, depending on what one wants the answer to be.

But it seems safe to conclude that as of 1989 the British underclass is still small enough not to represent nearly the problem that it does in the US. If the crime and illegitimacy trends in Britain magically level off where they are now and then the tight labour market that the south now enjoys spreads to the north, Britain would continue to have an underclass but not one that would force major reform. Britain could continue to treat social policy as it has since the

Beveridge Report of 1942, looking for ways to fine-tune a social welfare and criminal justice system that most Britons think works pretty well.

The question facing Britain is the same, haunting question facing the United States: how contagious is this disease? Is it going to spread indefinitely, or will it be self-containing?

Suppose, for example, that the trends continue unabated, and try to imagine Britain 10 years from now. The results seem preposterous. If violent crime follows the steepening trendline it has displayed since 1969, by 1999 your violent crime rate will be double the rate that already is a source of such concern. In the case of illegitimacy, it is impossible to assume that the exponential curve in the trendline since 1970 will continue to steepen— if it were to do so, all British births would be illegitimate by the end of the century. But even if we assume more conservatively that the trend of the past 10 years will continue linearly, more than 40 per cent of births will be to single women by 1999. Because these results are so obviously preposterous, the question arises: why might these projections be too high? Why may we reasonably expect that recent trends are caused by abnormal forces that are about to fade?

Questions about Causation

Here we reach controversial questions about causation. Frank Field, in his book on the emergence of a British underclass, *Losing Out,*[3] has no difficulty laying the blame at Mrs Thatcher's door. The organising principle for Field's analysis is inequality. The Thatcherites have rewarded the rich and punished the poor, increased inequalities, and hence (I am greatly simplifying an argument worth reading) Britain has a growing underclass. Change the policies, and the underclass will diminish.

My interpretation and those of the Left do not so much compete as pass in the night. As far as I can tell, inequality in general and Mrs Thatcher's policies in particular hardly enter in. The increases in crime extend back to the 1950s, and the slope in the graph in violent crime steepened most conspicuously in the late 1960s, long before Mrs Thatcher came to power. The acceleration in the illegitimacy ratio was taking off in 1979, and was as nearly as steep as it would ever get by Mrs Thatcher's first full year in office. It is hard to credit that Mrs Thatcher's influence on fertility behaviour among single young women occurred within days of her election.

In any case, let me propose a more radical reason why the Thatcher Government's policies have little to do with the development of an underclass: the relevant policies haven't changed that much under Mrs Thatcher. Despite the many dramatic changes in Britain in other spheres, the culprits behind the trends I have described have been largely unaffected.

I am recasting a version of the Right's view of why things go wrong that is usually expressed in terms of the decay of moral standards, the perverse incentives of welfare policy and the coddling of criminals. The problem with those arguments as they are usually presented is that they are too mechanistic. I do not believe women read about the latest change in the benefit rules for unwed mothers and use a pocket calculator to decide whether to get pregnant, or that young men decide whether to rob the local building society on the basis of a favourable change in parole policy.

Let us think instead in more common-sense terms. The topic is young people in their late teens and early twenties. The proposition is as simple as this: young people—not just poor young people, but all young people—try to make sense of the world around them. They behave in ways that reflect what they observe. In the 1960s and 1970s social policy in Britain fundamentally changed what makes sense. The changes did not affect the mature as much as the young. They affected the affluent hardly at all. Rather: the rules of the game changed fundamentally for low-income young people. Behaviour changed along with the changes in the rules.

'Making sense of the world around them' has to be understood in terms of the judgement and the time frame of the young person. Late adolescence is a critical time of life for shaping the future, and unfortunately also a time during which people are prone to do things that are foolish and self-destructive in the long term.

Crime Has Become Safer

Consider how the world was changing at the time when the trend-lines in crime and illegitimacy were changing. I begin with crime, assuming this common-sense view of the situation: if the chances that one will get punished for a crime go down, then crime goes up. In every respect—the chances of getting caught, the chances of being found guilty and the chances of going to prison—crime has become dramatically safer in Britain throughout the post-war period, and most blatantly safer since 1960.

Clear-up rates provide an example. With a few crimes such as homicide, the clear-up rate has remained high and unchanged. But for a crime such as robbery, the clear-up rate has fallen from 61 per cent in 1960 to 21 per cent in 1987—an extremely large change. Reductions for other crimes have been smaller but significant.

If clear-up rates had been the only thing to change, then the overall effect on the 'safeness' of crime would have been modest. But at the same time as clear-up rates were falling, so was the likelihood that one would be convicted for a crime even if caught. In 1960, 50 per cent of all cleared-up offences resulted in a conviction. By 1987, this proportion had fallen to 30 per cent.

Perhaps most importantly, the penalties imposed upon those convicted changed. This last topic is a source of great misunderstanding, for prison is the most obvious form of punishment and prisons are commonly accepted to be useless for reducing crime. Partly, the misunderstanding arises from a confusion between the limitations of prisons in rehabilitating people (which is reasonably well-documented) and the nature of the deterrent effect of prisons on potential offenders (which is not). Strict and consistent use of prisons, as once characterised Britain, can at the same time be miserably inefficient at rehabilitating criminals and spectacularly effective in deterring people from becoming criminals in the first place.

Another misunderstanding lies in the tendency of people to think in terms of the raw number of people in prison. As the number of prisoners rises but crime also continues to rise, the conclusion is loudly proclaimed that it doesn't do any good to incarcerate people. But if one is thinking in terms of risks, the obvious measure is not the number of people in prison, but rather the chances of going to prison if one commits a crime. That figure has plummeted. Prison sentences as a proportion of reported crimes fell by half during the period 1950 to 1970, and the 1970 figure had fallen again by half by 1987.

But comparatively few offenders were sent to prison even in the tough old days. This statistic may be treated as an example, not the whole story. 'Penalty' doesn't mean simply 'prison', nor even 'the judge's sentence'. Swiftness, certainty, consistency, and comparative severity of penalties are also important. A full analysis of the trends in punishment would consider fines as well as prison sentences; the use of cautions and suspended sentences; the effects of the parole system on actual time served; the delay between arrest and disposition; and a host of other factors that affect how a person arrested for a given crime in 1950 was treated differently from a person arrested for the same offence today. It seems evident from descriptions in the press and essays on the criminal justice system that the use of penalties has fallen in every dimension— not just severity, but swiftness and certainty, too.

The Use of Penalties has fallen

Even using simple measures, recent trends in penalties are at odds with the reputation of the Thatcher Government as tough, anti-crime and punitive. From 1982 to 1987, even as crime continued to rise, the number of convictions and prison sentences dropped— not just as a proportion of crimes, but in raw numbers. In 1982, 3.3 million indictable offences were known to the police, 475,000 persons were found guilty of them; of these, 50,300 received unsuspended prison sentences. In 1987, 3.9 million indictable offences were known to the police (up to 19 per cent), 386,000 were found guilty of them (down 19 per cent); of these, 41,700 received unsuspended prison sentences (down 17 per cent). People who use the past few years as evidence that a 'get rough' policy doesn't work aren't defining 'get tough' from the criminal's point of view.

Because crime statistics are so subject to qualifications (including the ones just presented—some form of 'immediate custody' for violent crimes went up during this period, for example) and punishment itself is a subject of such great passion, let me make clear what I am and am not saying. I'm not claiming that the police have become lax (they've been overwhelmed), nor that one must ignore the complicated social forces associated with increases in crime. Just this: committing a crime has been getting safer for more than three decades, and the trend continues today. That being the case, why shouldn't crime continue to increase? In fact, why shouldn't the slope in the graph of violent crime continue just as steeply upwards for the next 10 years? It might flatten out, but it is difficult to think of a good reason why.

Similarly, why shouldn't illegitimacy continue to increase? There is an obvious explanation for why single young women get pregnant: sex is fun and babies endearing. Nothing could be more natural than for young men and women to want to have sex, and nothing could be more natural than for a young woman to want a baby. A better question than asking why single young women get pregnant is to ask why they don't. The obvious answer is that in the past it was very punishing for a single woman to have a baby. (If that seems too negative, then one may say that a young single woman who had a baby had to forego many social and economic rewards.)

Social Stigma and Illegitimacy

One type of punishment was social stigma (or one type of reward for virtue was social acceptance), and without doubt the sexual revolution of the 1960s markedly reduced the stigma. Leaving aside the subtle question of why this happened, it is reasonable to expect that illegitimacy would have risen in the 1960s even if social policy had remained unchanged. But in addition to stigma, there was, historically, severe economic punishment awaiting single mothers. For a poor single woman, supporting a baby alone was next to impossible. Getting into that situation was something actively to be avoided.

The Benefit System

At this point we come to the benefit system, and another source of great controversy and confusion. Conservatives in particular often misconstrue the problem, railing against the woman who goes out and gets pregnant so that she can get on the dole. It happens occasionally but, as far as anyone knows, the reason why single young women have babies is seldom specifically so that they can get income benefits. (Sometimes they have a second child specifically so that they can remain on benefit, but that constitutes a comparatively minor part of the problem.)

Rather, the problem in providing money to single women is that the income enables many young women to do something they would naturally like to do. Such benefits don't have much effect on affluent women—the benefit rate is so far below what they consider their needs, that they are not in any way 'enabled' to have babies by the level of support being provided. For poor women, however, the benefit level can be quite salient in deciding whether having a baby is feasible. And the simple economic feasibility of raising a baby without the support of a father has changed fundamentally since the end of the Second World War.

In 1955, for example, an unmarried, unemployed mother with a single child under five had to get along on less than £22 a week in 1987 purchasing power, miserably little. It was almost impossible to survive on such a budget. Unless the mother had some other source of support, the only realistic option was putting the child up for adoption or into the care of the local authority. Having an illegitimate baby was brutally punishing if you were poor. (It was also punishing if you were rich, but for different reasons.) During the 1960s the benefit grew, reaching about £36 in 1987 purchasing power by 1970—still a slender stipend, though conceivably enough to get by on.

The Homeless Persons Act

During the first half of the 1970s the size of the benefit for single women began to rise more rapidly, increasing more than a third in purchasing power from 1970 to 1976. Then, in 1977, the Homeless Persons Act was passed. Before, a single mother had to wait in a queue for housing, but the new act stipulated that pregnant women and single mothers must get some sort of housing immediately—and go to the top of the queue for council housing—if they could demonstrate to the local authority's satisfaction that they couldn't live with their parents and were otherwise homeless.

I doubt that the Homeless Persons Act bribed many young women to have babies so that they could get their own flats. Rather, the increases in the benefits and the Homeless Persons Act were steps in a quiet, commonsensical, cumulative process whereby having a baby as a single mother went from 'extremely punishing' to 'not so bad'. By 1977, poor young women looking at the world around them could see that single mothers in their neighbourhoods were getting along, whereas a similar young woman in the 1950s would have looked around and concluded that single motherhood was an awful state to be in. The combination of cash and housing was not a package large enough to appeal to the middle class, but for a low-income young woman it provided a standard of living no worse and often better than she endured living with her parents. Meanwhile, sex was as fun as ever and babies were as endearing as ever. By the end of 1978 (one is tempted to add, beginning within the next nine months), the illegitimacy ratio had begun the rapid rise that has continued throughout the 1980s.

Once again, on this most inflammatory issue, let me be explicit about what I'm *not* saying. I'm not saying that single young women get pregnant for the money. I'm not chiding them for immorality. I'm not saying that they don't love their babies. I'm not saying that a 10 per cent cut in benefits will mean a 10 per cent reduction (or any reduction) in fertility among single women. Rather, a series of changes in the benefit rates and collateral housing benefits lifted a large portion of low-income young women above the threshold where having and keeping a baby became economically feasible.

It doesn't make any difference if the benefit level stops getting higher, or even if it diminishes somewhat. As long as the benefit level is well above the threshold, the dynamics of social incentives will continue to work in favour of illegitimacy as over time the advantages of legal marriage become less clear and its disadvantages more obvious. For men, the pressures to marry will continue to diminish. Given all this, I cannot see why the illegitimacy ratio should start to level off. It hasn't done so among poor people in the United States, where the illegitimacy ratio among blacks is now over 60 per cent. Why should poor whites in Britain be any different?

Social Problems are Interconnected

These changes in the law enforcement and benefit systems are not occurring in isolation. State education was a lively topic of conversation among people with whom I talked everywhere: the stories sounded depressingly like the problems with urban public education in the United States. Drug abuse in Britain is reported to be increasing significantly. Everything interacts. When one leaves school without any job skills, barely literate, the job alternatives to crime or having a baby or the dole are not attractive. Young men who are subsisting on crime or the dole are not likely to be trustworthy providers, which makes having a baby without a husband a more practical alternative. If a young man's girl friend doesn't need him to help support the baby, it makes less sense for him to plug away at a menial job and more sense to have some fun—which in turn makes hustling and crime more attractive, marriage less attractive. Without a job or family to give life meaning, drugs become that much more valuable as a means of distraction. The cost of drugs makes crime the only feasible way to make enough money to pay for them. The interconnections go on endlessly, linking up with the reasons why community norms change, the role of older adults in the community changes, community bonds change.

Incremental Changes Won't Solve the Problem

The implication of these interconnections is that modest, incremental changes in one corner of the system are unlikely to have much effect. Everybody's pet solutions are wrong. People on the Right who think that they can reduce illegitimacy by snipping benefits are wrong. (Illegitimacy would be cut radically if you slashed benefits back to the 1970 level, but that's not under consideration.) The notion that giving the police more latitude or legislating longer prison sentences will reduce crime is wrong. (Crime would be cut radically if you enforced laws as strictly as you did in 1950, but in the short term that would mean tripling your prison population and vastly expanding your court system.)

People on the Left who think things will get better when Labour comes back to power are just as wrong. The accepted wisdom on the Left is that all this is the fault of the Thatcher Government, the soaring unemployment that began in the late 1970s, and an ethos of greed and individualism. An American familiar with the history of the 1960s in the United States is slow to buy that explanation. There, the surge in crime and illegitimacy and drop-out from the labour force coincided with the ascendancy of the Left and with prosperity.

This imponderable remains: what will happen if jobs do become plentiful everywhere? In the United States, the experts are still trying to come to terms with what has become too obvious to ignore. Throughout the 1970s, the conventional wisdom on the Left was that scarcity of jobs was the root problem and the provision of jobs was the root solution. But during the past five years, several American cities have enjoyed red-hot economies, with low-skill jobs paying good wages easily available. The evidence is accumulating that this economic growth is having almost no effect on the size of the underclass. Many of the dropouts don't even want such jobs—they are 'demeaning' because they are menial, 'chump change' even if they pay $5 or $6 an hour. Others say they want jobs, and apply for them, then stop showing up after a few days. Or they get into fights with their co-workers and supervisors and are fired, because they cannot deal with the discipline of the workplace.

Once jobs become available, will the young British males who have been shut out of the labour force come flocking back? Some will, but others won't, and, in counting them, Britain will begin to get some idea of how large the underclass has become.

What Can Britain Learn from the American Experience?

Britain is not the United States, and the most certain of predictions is that the British experience will play out differently from the US experience. At the close of this brief tour of several huge topics, I will be the first to acknowledge that I have skipped over complications and nuances and certainly missed all sorts of special British conditions of which I am ignorant. Still, so much has been the same so far. In both countries, the same humane impulses and the same intellectual fashions drove the reforms in social policy. The attempts to explain away the consequences have been similar, with British intellectuals in the 1980s saying the same things that American intellectuals were saying in the 1970s about how the problems aren't really as bad as they seem.

So if the United States has had so much more experience with a growing underclass, what can Britain learn from it? The sad answer is—not much. The central truth that the politicians in the United States are unwilling to face is our powerlessness to deal with an underclass once it exists. No matter how much money we spend on our cleverest social interventions, we don't know how to turn around the lives of teenagers who have grown up in an underclass culture. Providing educational opportunities or job opportunities doesn't do it. Training programmes don't reach the people who need them most. We don't know how to make up for the lack of good parents—day-care doesn't do it, foster homes don't work very well. Most of all, we don't know how to make up for the lack of a community that rewards responsibility and stigmatises irresponsibility.

Let me emphasise the words: we *do not know how*. It's not money we lack, but the capability to social-engineer our way out of this situation. Unfortunately, the delusion persists that our social engineering simply hasn't been clever enough, and that we must strive to become more clever.

Authentic Self-Government is the Key

The alternative I advocate is to have the central government stop trying to be clever and instead get out of the way, giving poor communities (and affluent communities, too) a massive dose of self-government, with vastly greater responsibility for the operation of the institutions that affect their lives—including the criminal justice, educational, housing and benefit systems in their localities. My premise is that it is unnatural for a neighbourhood to tolerate high levels of crime or illegitimacy or voluntary idleness among its youth: that, given the chance, poor communities as well as rich ones will run affairs so that such things happen infrequently. And when communities with different values run their affairs differently, I want to make it as easy as possible for people who share values to live together. If people in one neighbourhood think marriage is an outmoded institution, fine; let them run their neighbourhood as they see fit. But make it easy for the couple who thinks otherwise to move into a neighbourhood where two-parent families are valued. There are many ways that current levels of expenditure for public systems could be sustained (if that is thought to be necessary) but control over them decentralised. Money isn't the key. Authentic self-government is.

But this is a radical solution, and the explanation of why it might work took me 300 pages the last time I tried. In any case, no one in either the United States or Britain is seriously contemplating such steps. That leaves both countries with similar arsenals of social programmes which don't work very well, and the prospect of an underclass in both countries that not only continues but grows.

Oddly, this does not necessarily mean that the pressure for major reforms will increase. It is fairly easy to propitiate the consciences of the well-off and pacify rebellion among the poor with a combination of benefits and social programmes that at least employ large numbers of social service professionals. Such is the strategy that the United States has willy-nilly adopted. Even if the underclass is out there and still growing, it needn't bother the rest of us too much as long as it stays in its own part of town. Everybody's happy—or at least not so unhappy that more action has to be taken.

The Bleak Message

So, Britain, that's the bleak message. Not only do you have an underclass, not only is it growing, but, judging from the American experience, there's not much in either the Conservative or Labour agendas that has a chance of doing anything about it. A few years ago I wrote for an American audience that the real contest about social policy is not between people who want to cut budgets and people who want to help. Watching Britain replay our history, I can do no better than repeat the same conclusion. When meaningful reforms finally do occur, they will happen not because stingy people have won, but because generous people have stopped kidding themselves.

Notes

1   Vol. 16, No. 3, pp. 293-318.

2   Hall, S. *et al.*, *Policing the Crisis,* London: Macmillan, 1978.

3   Field, F., *Losing Out: The Emergence of Britain's Underclass,* Oxford: Blackwell, 1989.

Figure 1
Births to Single Women as a Percentage of All Births

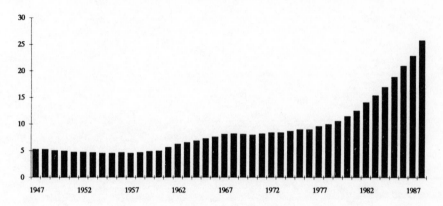

Figure 2
Crimes of Violence per 100,000 Population

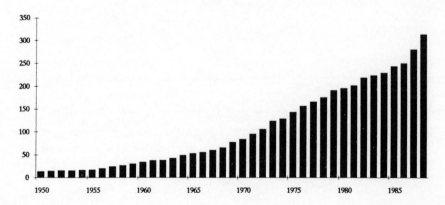

Commentaries

Britain's Underclass: Countering the Growth

Frank Field MP

Charles Murray's work illustrates both the advantage and disadvantage of looking in at somebody else's country. His advantage is to bring a new pair of eyes when examining a social landscape which others have become tired of describing. But the fresh pair of eyes have been trained to look at the American terrain and so there is the danger of trying to transpose an American vision onto Britain.

Some commentators will no doubt have fun in writing good knocking copy against Murray's view. His errors of fact, or unusualness of interpretation, should not blind anyone to Murray's main message. He seeks to show that something new is happening in Britain and that an underclass is emerging here as assuredly as it is prominent in American society.

As I have attempted to set out in *Losing Out: the Emergence of Britain's Underclass,* I accept that Britain does now have a group of poor people who are so distinguished from others on low income that it is appropriate to use the term 'underclass' to describe their position in the social hierarchy.[1]

A Racial Phenomenon

It is, however, necessary at the outset to distinguish a fundamental difference between British and American society. The difference is clearly expressed in Nicholas Lemann's influential contribution to the American debate. Writing in the *Atlantic Monthly* he portrays an underclass largely as a racial phenomenon. Lemann writes that the:

> underclass did not just spring into being over the past twenty years. Every aspect of the underclass culture in the ghetto is directly traceable to roots in the South—not the South of slavery, but the South of a generation ago. In fact, there seems to be a strong correlation between the underclass status in the North, and the family background in the nascent underclass of the share-cropper South.[2]

There is no racial basis to Britain's underclass. To be sure, many blacks are to be found in its ranks, but they are there because they occupy some of the most vulnerable positions in British society. Where there are no blacks—such as in Birkenhead—the underclass is composed exclusively of poor whites.

This distinction between the two countries is also important for the prescriptive part of any debate on Britain's underclass. Too much of American literature—and Charles Murray is guilty here—employs a 'culture of poverty' interpretation of the underclass's advent. While it is important that the attitudes of the poor are considered, they do not by themselves give an adequate understanding as to why this new social phenomenon has occurred.

Structural Causes of the Underclass

In Britain it is important to begin with emphasising the structural causes of the underclass. I see this group composed of three groups; the very frail, elderly pensioner, the single parent with no chance of escaping welfare under the existing rules and with prevailing attitudes, and the long-term unemployed.

Pensioner income has recently risen substantially. But not all pensioners have benefited from the major increases in the real value of occupational pensions. Elderly pensioners, by and large, are those without a private pension and are overwhelmingly much the poorer. This group has been particularly hard hit by the present Government's decision to break the link between state pensions and the rise in earnings or prices—taking whichever is the most favourable to pensioners. This action, which reversed the Macmillan Government's decision to tie in the living standards of those on welfare with rising prosperity, is more responsible than any other action in economically cutting this group off from other groups, and recruiting it into the underclass. No-one in their right mind believes that this group has volunteered for membership.

Single-Parent Families and the Unemployed

The position is somewhat different in respect of single-parent families and the unemployed. There is no question that the vast majority of both of these two groups initially viewed membership of the underclass with disdain. But once in the underclass, attitudes have changed. Countering the growth in the underclass amongst these two groups requires new policies and determination.

The fastest growing group on welfare is single mothers. Amongst this group, the biggest increase is now in very young single mothers. In countering this trend it is crucial that young girls in school should learn from young single mothers that having a baby does result in jumping the housing queue, but only as far as the first sink council estate. Similarly, young males need to learn that the state will hold them responsible for the maintenance of their children. Maintenance orders attached to the man's national insurance record would ensure that today's dodge—of constantly changing jobs so that the mother has to go back to court for a new attachment of earnings—becomes pointless.

Full Employment UK

The pioneering work that Full Employment UK has undertaken amongst the unemployed shows how much more difficult it is going to be to encourage back into mainstream society the disillusioned young unemployed worker. Of course, in areas of high unemployment there are large numbers of people willing to take almost any job.

But that is not true in areas where the labour market is tight. Some of these unemployed young workers use the Government's Employment Training schemes merely to win more time on welfare rather than as an entry into the labour market. Many, too, have criminal records which make the prospect of gaining employment a near impossibility—unless one has an amnesty on such criminal records. Many of this group now simply despise those who are on the inside of the labour market in low-paid jobs.

Enforcing fairly an availability-for-work test is crucial so that people do take work when it is available. Without the structure that work gives to our day, many people's lives simply disintegrate. It is here, however, that the needs of the unemployed underclass and the low paid are identical. As a policy of reinforcing the position of those who are playing by society's rules in the labour market it is crucial that training is personalised. Without this, many low-paid workers will be trapped with employers who not only pay badly but who resolutely refuse to give workers the chance of exiting from low-paid jobs by increasing their skills.

The personal approach to training will similarly be required by many of today's unemployed. Full Employment UK has advocated the introduction of personalised training accounts, the value of which is built up from the worker himself, his employer and the Government. The introduction of such accounts would make the policing of existing training programmes that much less important. Workers, realising what a bad deal they are getting, and knowing that the course will be paid from their own training accounts, will vote with their feet and enrol in other courses.

But this assumes that both the low paid and the unemployed have a clear idea of their own skills, their potential, and likely changes in the labour market over the coming decade. The employment service needs to begin behaving as though it believed in its title. The building up of career advisers will also play a crucial part in a transformed employment service.

A Comprehensive Approach

A comprehensive approach needs to knit together other policies too. But the watershed must be that more of the same sorts of policies will do little to prevent new groups from becoming disaffected, or to change the balance of advantage in joining society for those who have already been sectioned into Britain's underclass.

Notes

1   Field, F., *Losing Out: the Emergence of Britain's Underclass,* London: Blackwell, 1989.

2   Lemann, N., *Atlantic Monthly*, June 1986, p. 35.

The Focus on Single Mothers

Joan C. Brown

It is quite easy to put together a package of figures—all authentic—which creates a particular kind of picture of one-parent families, 90 per cent of whom are headed by a woman. They form a growing proportion of all families with children, up from 8 per cent in 1971 to 14 per cent in 1986 and 16 per cent in 1988. The numbers have risen from 570,000 in 1971 to over one million in 1986. The rate of births outside marriage has also increased, from 8 per cent in 1971 to 21 per cent in 1986 and 25 per cent in 1988.

The number of lone mothers on Supplementary Benefit (now Income Support) has gone up accordingly, from 238,000 in November 1971 to 578,000 in February 1986. In that month, some 93 per cent of single (never married) mothers were on SB, 95 per cent of separated mothers and 42 per cent of divorced mothers. Single mothers were the largest single group of lone mothers on benefit, 213,000 of them, followed by 180,000 separated wives and 172,000 divorced women. The balance were widows and wives of prisoners.

The available figures do not support what is apparently the assumption of some politicians, that 75 per cent of lone mothers are single never-married mothers. Although there is a proportionate increase in this group, as the number of widows has declined, they still constitute just over one-quarter of lone mothers, the dominant group being formerly married mothers. Nor can the idea that this is a 'black problem' be sustained—and here I agree with Charles Murray. A recent analysis by Haskey has shown that, while the proportion of one parent families among the ethnic minority population of West Indian origin is notably higher than among the white population, West Indian families constitute only one per cent of all families in Great Britain.[1] Their influence on the one-parent family figure is, therefore, minimal.

Still, the picture the figures present is of a growing population of one-parent families, mostly fatherless families, dependent on benefits to quite a staggering extent. Moreover, while in 1986, 50 per cent of married mothers went out to work to help support their families, only

42 per cent of lone mothers worked, and as few as 25 per cent of single mothers, and half of them part-time only. Such figures are often used to suggest a willingness, or even a preference to be dependent long term on state benefits, especially by single mothers.

The Misleading Nature of Statistics

But all of these statistics are point-in-time figures. They provide a snapshot of one-parent families at the end of one month in a year. Murray believes, arguing from US experience, that for single mothers, the picture is nevertheless substantially correct. But while the US did not produce figures separating welfare mothers into different categories until 1986, when single mothers were shown to spend far longer on welfare than other lone mothers, the DHSS has been publishing categorised figures for the duration spent on Supplementary Benefit going back to 1970. It is true that these do not show the sum of different spells on benefit—for example, of a lone mother who leaves benefit for work and then loses the job and has to reclaim— but the figures are, nevertheless, quite enlightening, and do not support Murray's thesis.

In 1981, of those on benefit, 7.8 per cent of single mothers and 9.6 per cent of divorced mothers had been on SB for more than 10 years, and 15.6 per cent of single and 27.4 per cent of divorced mothers had been on benefit for 5-9 years, giving a five years plus total for 23 per cent of single mothers and 37 per cent of the divorced mothers. By 1987 (when only five years plus figures were published), 27 per cent of single mothers were this long on benefit and 37 per cent of divorced mothers. The duration on benefit of single mothers has increased—a trend that may in part be attributed to high unemployment in the 1980s—but, as a group, they still tend to spend shorter periods on benefit than divorced mothers, or indeed than widowed mothers. The lowest figure for more than 5 years duration is for separated wives, at 12.4 per cent, but many of these may simply transfer to another category on divorce.

Children Without Fathers

Murray is not only concerned about 'welfare dependency'. His central argument on single mothers is based on the undesirable effects on the children and on the community of the absence of fathers. The child of a single mother is 'without a father from day one' (he says) and the ensuing discussion implies that this child spends his or her whole childhood without a father. But the principal reason that single mothers do not spend long years as lone mothers on benefit is that they marry—and introduce a father into the household by so doing.

Ermisch has shown that single mothers end their lone parenthood through marriage faster than other lone parents.[2] Their median duration as single lone parents is 35 months, compared with 59 months for women who become lone parent through marriage breakdown. By the time the child is five years old, 60 per cent of single mothers have married, and 70 per cent by the time the child is seven years.

Ermisch's study was based on a large 1980 survey, and in 1990 may have to be modified. But the change is less likely to be a longer duration of fatherlessness, than an increase in cohabitation rather than marriage. It is a change that may also be reducing remarriage rates after divorce and widowhood. Among women aged 18-49, with and without children, the proportion cohabiting has risen from nine per cent of single women and 39 per cent of divorced and separated women in 1981, to 20 per cent of single and 52 per cent of divorced and separated women in 1988.[3]

Given these patterns, pointing the finger at single mothers—but not at divorced or separated wives—as an especial danger to society makes little sense. If, for a child, being brought up without a father is of key importance, it is hard to see a difference of major social significance between starting life without a father and then acquiring one, and starting life with a father and then losing him, even though it might have been better for the child in both cases if there had been a stable union involving both natural parents.

Neighbourhoods of Lone Mothers

Moreover, Murray's picture of whole neighbourhoods dominated by lone mothers has to be looked at twice. It is undesirable that housing policies, both national and local, have resulted in the undue concentration of one-parent families in poor neighbourhoods, often in the least desirable property. But this says more about our treatment of one-parent families than about the 'contaminating' influence of single mothers. In any case, the one-parent families in the area cannot all be single mothers. And since many lone mothers will marry or, in the case of divorced and widowed mothers, remarry, they cannot be judged to be offering an example of a permanent rejection of marriage or of the role of men in families.

Murray's thesis may have been exaggerated for effect, so as to get his main point over, but making scapegoats of single mothers for society's ills does not help us to approach the serious issues raised by the growing proportion of one-parent families. This growth has to be seen in the context of changes in social attitudes across the wider society. We live in an age when (according to the British Social Attitudes Survey for 1983) over 90 per cent of those aged between 18 and 34 do not consider pre-marital sex to be particularly wrong, and when divorce and cohabitation are increasing and are being seen as acceptable at all levels of society. We may want to seek ways to counter these developments at an individual level, but is not easy to see how we can turn back the clock to a less permissive age—short of a massive religious revival or draconian laws which attempt to control private behaviour between adults.

'Back to the Past'

Nor is it easy to see the practicality of the 'back to the past' solution of social reorganisation based on local community empowerment. Even if a local community could exercise any substantial control over its own affairs in a free market economy, where decisions taken outside the community and sometimes thousands of miles away can destroy its economic base—and at times its social base also—and within a housing market in which housing mobility is reserved for those with ample resources, there would have to be doubts about such a solution to the issues raised by one-parent families. Local control may have advantages in many spheres, but past experience suggests that it also involves harsh and unjust decisions to punish and exclude those judged—by those exercising local influence and power—as undesirable.

The solution Murray does not recommend—though he obviously hankers after—is to make severe cuts in benefits for lone mothers. But, for my part, I have never seen the social morality of storming the barricades over the bodies of living children. The reform of our society ought not to require the sacrifice of the 1.6 million children currently in one-parent families.

Reducing Welfare Dependence

The reality is that, practically and ethically, we have to start from where we are. That means we have to be prepared to put effort and resources into programmes aimed at strengthening the two-parent family—if only because the breakdown of relationships, whether before or during marriage, creates so much unhappiness for parents and children. But we must also seek to strengthen the ability of one-parent families to offer their children a sound family life, for as long as they hold that status. And we need policies which neither discourage marriage or remarriage, nor put on economic pressure to enter new unions which have an obvious risk of failure, given the increasing level of second divorces involving children.

If we want to reduce welfare dependence, and ensure that lone mothers are not isolated from society and from general community life and values, then we have to tackle the obstacles that prevent lone mothers from combining home responsibilities and the interests of the children with paid employment. And we have to deal with another major problem—not mentioned by Murray—the large scale failure of absent fathers to meet their responsibilities for the support of their children. That means facing up to the need for a substantial reform of the maintenance system.

Finally, it ought to be said that Murray is right to argue that all the social trends he described began before 1979. But he is wrong to exonerate a Government which has been in power for over ten years, claims to be the party of the family, but has signally failed to address the need for a coherent and properly resourced family policy.

Notes

1 John Haskey, 'Families and Households of Ethnic Minority and White Populations of Great Britain', *Population Trends*, Vol. 57, Autumn 1989, pp. 8-19.

2 Ermisch, J., 'The *Economics of the Family: Applications to Divorce and Remarriage*', *Discussion Paper* No. 40, CEPR, London, 1986.

3 'General Household Survey: Preliminary Results for 1988',*OPCS Monitor*, 5 December 1989.

Blaming the Victims

Alan Walker

In virtually every decade this century a concerted attempt has been made in Britain to separate two groups of poor people: those whose poverty is caused by factors largely beyond their control and those whose behaviour contributes in large measure to their own poverty. The proposition that this latter group poses a threat to the social order often lurks somewhere in this sort of analysis (and, as Nicholas Deakin points out, this apocalyptic variation on the underclass thesis has been advanced by both extremes of the political spectrum). In the dying weeks of the last decade Charles Murray made a serious bid for the role of social policy Cassandra of the 1980s, a role that he had already secured in the US.

In fact, as Murray suggests, the distinction between deserving and undeserving poor goes back much further, at least 500 years in this country. It is particularly favoured by the political Right because it panders to their underlying belief in individual responsibility and minimum intervention by the state in welfare. Thus it was no surprise at all to find Murray, one of the champions of the 1980s neo-liberal thinking on social policy in the US, staking his claim. What was surprising, perhaps, was that he did so with such conviction in a country where, in his own words, he is ignorant of 'all sorts of special conditions'. Despite this the conclusion he reaches is unequivocal: Britain has an underclass and it is growing rapidly.

There are two main deficiencies to Murray's thesis. In the first place he fails to provide any scientific proof that an underclass exists. Substituting for such evidence are innuendos, assertions and anecdotes. Secondly, as a guide to policy, his thesis is, at best, misleading and, at worst, a dangerous diversion from the major problems of poverty and deprivation facing Britain.

In Search of the Underclass

The essence of Murray's argument is that an underclass consists of not necessarily the poorest people, but those of a different type who behave differently not just from the middle-class but, crucially, from other poor people as well. They define themselves as different, in Murray's terms, by their parenting, criminal and labour market behaviour, though there is no scientific justification for the selection of these particular criteria nor for the change in behaviour that is supposed to take place when benefits rise above a certain 'threshold'. Thus, stripped to its bare essentials, it is the poor that are to blame for their poverty because they choose to act in certain deviant ways or are conditioned to do so.

In social policy and practical terms, the belief that some poor people are poor because they do not conform to prevailing social values and therefore need to be disciplined may be traced from the repression of vagrancy under the Elizabethan Poor Law, to the workhouse test of the 1834 Poor Law Amendment Act, to the 1930s genuinely-seeking-work test, to the voluntary unemployment rules, YTS and Restart programmes of the 1980s.

A similar legacy may be traced, in intellectual and research terms, from the beginning of this century. Early theories concerning social pathology were heavily influenced by eugenicists, with both official and independent studies being conducted into the inheritance of physical and mental defects. With characteristic foresight Barbara Wootton's critique of this research tradition provided a rebuttal of Murray's piece exactly 30 years before he wrote it.[1] For instance there is his methodological failure to test the permanence or otherwise of underclass status and, especially, his failure to distinguish between the impact of personal inadequacy and simple economic misfortune. In the late 1950s attention turned from biological to cultural transmission. First, in the USA, researchers such as Oscar Lewis examined lower-class slum settlements in cities like San Juan and concluded that there was a culture of poverty distinct from poverty. Lewis' work has been the subject of conclusive scientific criticisms—including its lack of representativeness, the absence of specification or quantification of the sub-culture, internal contradictions and the impossibility of testing the thesis—several of which may be applied with equal force to Murray's analysis. Britain's variation on the culture of poverty thesis was the 'cycle of deprivation' first put forward by none other than Sir Keith Joseph, in a pre-Thatcherite guise, back in 1972. The central idea was that poverty persists because social problems reproduce themselves from one generation to the next and, specifically, that inadequate parents tend to rear inadequate children.

Mr Murray's thesis fits very neatly into this ideological and theoretical legacy, with its characteristic mixture of popular stereotypes, prejudice about the causes of poverty and ill-founded quasi-scientific notions. It is indicative that the language Murray uses to describe the underclass echoes the medical models of the past: 'disease', 'plague', 'contamination'. However, it is with the bold statement 'the underclass does not refer to degree of poverty, but to a type of poverty' that he squarely identifies himself with this approach. Thus he not only separates a type of poor person from others but also personalises the causes of this type of poverty, with a strong whiff of the public accusations of fault and attribution of stigma associated with past eras. His explanation of underclass poverty represents a blend of both cultural and cycle of deprivation elements, including parenting behaviour and contamination by association.

Is There an Underclass?

This approach to poverty, of which Charles Murray's rather idiosyncratic notion of an underclass is but the latest variation, has already been demolished by the overwhelming weight of scientific evidence against it. For example, didn't anyone tell Mr Murray that Sir Keith Joseph prompted a massive research programme in the 1970s devoted to his then pet theory: nearly £1 million, 37 different studies producing 20 books and a mountain of papers. One of the main findings of this programme was that there is no simple continuity of social problems between generations of the sort implied then by Joseph and now by Murray.

> At least half of the children born into a disadvantaged home do not repeat the pattern of disadvantage in the next generation. Over half of all forms of disadvantage arise anew each generation.[2]

Or, as the final report on this programme put it, 'continuities are by no means inevitable and there is no general sense in which "like begets like"'.[3] As Murray knows, very similar findings emerged from the research on the American War on Poverty in the late 1960s.

What this research and a vast amount of subsequent scientific work shows is *not* that poor people are alienated from society, have different values or behave differently (when we allow for the devastating impact that poverty has on behaviour) but, rather, their remarkable assimilation into the attitudes, values and aspirations of

British society. There is plenty of contemporary research evidence. Murray singles out a supposed difference between younger and older people in attitudes towards employment as one of the three legs of his case. But, contrary to his anecdotes, a recent representative study of young long-term unemployed men and women found that they placed very great importance on having jobs.

> This was demonstrated by their continued search for employment in the face of repeated failure and disappointment, and in their willingness to stay in jobs which were poorly-paid or otherwise unattractive just to avoid further unemployment... In interview after interview, the advice these young people offered themselves, and others like them, was to *keep looking, don't give up.*[4]

Murray's data on economic activity are from 1981, the height of the last recession in Britain when school-leavers faced unemployment rates of up to 50 per cent. (The recession itself and the surge of unemployment that resulted from it was, in large part, the result of the government's own policies.) Research among the 'aristocracy' of skilled labour in Sheffield during this period, the fathers of the young people Murray criticises, showed how even their commitment to employment was ground down by the sheer hopelessness of their search for work.[5] Is it any surprise that, during this period, young people quickly learnt the reality of the labour market from their fathers before they themselves faced it? Furthermore, the fact that some young people reject YTS places is not sufficient to attribute deviant status to them—many such schemes *are* slave labour and the programme has a notoriously poor safety record (a fatal accident rate of 138.2 per 100,000 trainees)—unless, that is, membership of the underclass is determined solely on the basis of Mr Murray's or Mrs Thatcher's values.

As far as the main element of his case is concerned—the growth of illegitimacy—the evidence similarly offers him little comfort. (As it happens the legal concept of illegitimacy was abolished by the Family Law Reform Act, 1987.) The latest official figures show that at least half of the children born outside marriage in 1986, in fact, had parents who were living together.[6] In other words, the union may not have been sanctified by marriage but the children were living within a stable family, with a father. This simply demonstrates, among other things, that attitudes towards marriage are changing. This conclusion is backed-up by figures on conceptions among people under the age of 20. While the proportion of such births inside marriage halved between 1975 and 1985, the proportion outside marriage but jointly registered rose by three times. Some three out of five illegitimate births to women under 20 are jointly registered.

This is not to suggest that illegitimacy should not be regarded as a social issue but rather that Mr Murray has got it a little out of proportion. The illegitimacy rate in Denmark is more than double Britain's and, as far as I know, that society is not on the brink of disaster. Moreover, in Britain the data show that marriage breakdown is the main cause of lone parenthood, not illegitimacy.

In the end it is not clear whether it is illegitimacy, as he says, or lone parenthood that worries Murray. Whichever it is, the prospect he conjures up of a plague of young single mothers contaminating whole neighbourhoods is, quite simply, ridiculous. As Joan Brown showed in her recent study of lone parents on benefit, Murray's image of young single mothers represents only a small minority of lone parents.

> If there is a typical lone parent, it is a separated or divorced woman. The children involved may be very young, but are more likely to be over 5 years...[7]

Murray does not mention the duration of lone parenthood status—surely a key variable for his underclass thesis? British research indicates that single, never-married women leave lone parenthood more quickly than divorced women: their median duration as lone parents is 35 months compared with 59 months for women who become lone parents as a result of marriage breakdown.[8]

If this sort of evidence is not sufficient to convince Mr Murray that he is barking up the wrong tree he need look no further than the case studies published alongside his article in *The Sunday Times Magazine*.[9] Purporting to be examples of life among the underclass in North Peckham what they actually illustrate are attitudes and values, for example, towards bringing-up children, that are more in tune with the rest of society than at odds with it.

So, there is no evidence of a separate type of poverty, still less of a sub-culture or sub-strata alienated from the rest of society and with different values from it, or of a process of transmission or contamination.

The Growing Divide

Let me be clear, I am not arguing that there is no problem and we have nothing to worry about. It is just that the research evidence compels me to see the issue completely differently from Mr Murray: the problem concerns the degree of poverty and not the type of poverty.

The problem of poverty, significant in the 1970s, has worsened substantially in the 1980s. At the same time, uniquely in postwar Britain, the slight trend towards a narrowing of differentials in income and wealth has been thrown into reverse. This has been a conscious act of Government policy, comprising, briefly, cuts in benefits for the poorest and cuts in taxation for the richest.[10] This has created a rapid and massive polarisation of living standards. At one extreme there is a severely deprived group whose behaviour is predictably influenced by their abject poverty but who still do not resemble an underclass in any sociological sense. The only reason they, in Murray's words, 'live in a different world' is that they have no choice. Some, for example, are lone parents who have been clustered together as an act of housing management.

At the other extreme are a growing number of very wealthy people (an 'overclass' Mr Murray?). As an act of social policy gross inequalities, unknown in Britain for at least 100 years, have been created. This polarisation brings with it segregation. Witness the building of security fences around some of the new private or privatised housing developments in London's docklands, so that the rich can live in a different world from the poor. This new segregation is being exacerbated by Government policies towards public welfare services, such as health and education, which have been cut back while the private sector has been subsidised; a policy designed to produce private affluence and public squalor.

These two extremes have been openly engineered by Government policy, and the massive inequalities underlying them are two parts of the same problem. To paraphrase Tawney, what thoughtful rich people may refer to as the problem of poverty thoughtful poor people may call the problem of wealth. Only the rose-tinted spectacles of neo-liberal ideological commitment could fail to see the adverse transformation that British society has undergone in the last decade of Thatcherism. The idea that the Government's social policies do not depart from those of previous governments is a crude attempt to avoid the compelling facts. Read the evidence, Mr Murray. For example, the Family Policy Studies Centre has just shown how Government income support policies are adversely affecting families and creating destitution among 16-18-year-olds.[11] The latest report from the National Association of Citizens Advice Bureaux catalogues the hardship and high levels of unmet need as poor families are refused money to buy the most basic and essential everyday items.[12] These are but recent examples of an overwhelming indictment of the Government's policies.

The Poverty of Mr Murray's Policies

This brings me to the other major defect of Murray's analysis: his policy conclusions. The cause of the problem is 'well meaning' (sic) government intervention; the answer is to remove the influence of government. This Alexandrian solution was set out at length in his book Losing Ground[13] but then, as now, there was no evidence that this would either help or at least not make things worse. It is, after all, incumbent on Murray to demonstrate that his radical solution would not repeat the horrors of earlier and contemporary free markets. The tyranny of the welfare state, as he sees it, could well be replaced by a far fiercer tyranny of various unfettered corporate or neighbourhood welfare states.

So what should be done? A policy to combat poverty and the increasing social polarisation of British society would include a significant redistribution of income from rich to poor, reversing the £50,000 million cut from the income tax of the top 10 per cent of wage earners since 1979 which has caused some of the problem; the 'universal' targeting of social security for example on families, through child benefit, and people with disabilities, through a comprehensive disability income scheme; and a minimum wage to ensure that the 'deserving' poor (who Murray strangely excluded from his account) are not exploited. A longer term strategy would seek to ensure that all of the nation's resources are geared more effectively to meeting need.[14] In addition measures must be taken to liberate poor people and other service (public and private) users from bureaucracy and excessive restrictions on their self-determination. Here our analyses touch fleetingly. However, I would pursue this empowerment through legal citizenship rights to welfare and employment which would, of course, be coupled with duties such as paid employment, caring and other forms of social reproduction.

Murray's Thesis is Misleading

Herein lies what is probably the most important shortcoming of Murray's thesis: it is misleading, perhaps wilfully so. It diverts attention, on the one hand, from the real problems: pauperization and social segregation as acts of Government policy. On the other hand, it misleads policy-makers and the general public into believing that poverty is a residual personal, family or neighbourhood issue, rather than a widespread one. This is a serious matter because arguments such as Murray's diminish the scale and complexity of the problem facing society in combating poverty, and encourage the belief that comparatively simple and inexpensive policies can be effective. Because it minimises the problem it is likely to be superficially attractive to people outside of Murray's ideological rut: it allows poverty to be acknowledged but does not imply that we should feel guilty about it. In other words, Mr Murray's underclass, like all previous attempts to individualise the causes of poverty, diverts our attention from blaming the mechanisms through which resources are distributed, including the role of the Government, to blaming, in William Ryan's famous phrase, 'the victims'.

Notes

1 Wootton,B., *Social Science and Social Pathology,* London: Allen & Unwin, 1959.

2 Rutter, M. and Madge, N., *Cycles of Disadvantage,* London: Heinemann, 1976, p. 304.

3 Brown, M. and Madge, N., *Despite the Welfare State,* London: Heinemann, 1982, p. 143.

4 McRae, S., *Young and Jobless,* London: Policy Studies Institute, 1987, p. 144.

5 Westergaard, J., Noble, I. and Walker, A., *After Redundancy,* Oxford: Polity Press 1989.

6 CSO, *Social Trends 1989,* London: HMSO, 1989, p. 47.

7 Brown, J., *Why Don't They Go to Work? Mothers on Benefit,* London: HMSO, 1989, p. 10.

8 Ermisch, J., *The Economics of the Family: Applications to Divorce and Remarriage,* London: CEPR, 1986.

9 *Sunday Times Magazine,* 26 November 1989.

10 Walker, A. and Walker, C, (eds.), *The Growing Divide,* London: CPAG, 1987.

11 Roll, J., *Young People: Growing Up in The Welfare State,* London: FPSC, 1990.

12 *Hard Times for Social Fund Applicants,* London: NACAB, 1990.

13 Murray, C., *Losing Ground,* New York: Basic Books, 1984.

14 The Sheffield Group, *The Social Economic and the Democratic State,* London: Lawrence and Wishart, 1989.

M ister Murray's Ark

Nicholas Deakin

FOR the second time in twenty years, the British social science community has received a peremptory summons to accept that an imminent crisis of the underclass is upon us. At the end of the 1960s it was younger Marxist critics who perceived inevitable conflict arising from the frustrated aspirations of an exploited sub-proletariat largely composed of immigrant workers; now it is Conservatives who warn us—in equally doomladen terms—of inevitable contamination of the values and standards of our society through the growth of a culturally distinct and undeserving urban lumpenproletariat. On each occasion, we have been told, our complacency has blinded us both to the true facts and the wrath to come.

Murray's Tripod

Well, as Mr Murray himself might put it, maybe so. But on this occasion, as on the last, the evidence that is being deployed strikes me as a mite less than wholly compelling. Murray's case for the existence of his version of the underclass phenomenon rests on a tripod—increases in numbers of 'illegitimate' births, rising crime rates and growth in unemployment—two legs of which are distinctly shaky. Take illegitimacy. This (in Murray's conception) represents 'the purest form of being without parents' and as such constitutes one of the sharpest hazards to the development of normal community life: it removes the male parent from the key role he should play in the developmental process through which responsible future citizens must pass. The difficulty with this concept—which Murray himself has to concede—is that half those born 'illegitimate' have their two parents living together at the time of birth; and that many of these relationships will in due course result in the marriage of the natural parents. Alternatively, their mother may either marry or cohabit with another man, thereby providing a surrogate male parent for her children. Why step-parents do not feature in Murray's account is a mystery, given the exceptionally rapid growth over the last decade of families that are thus 'reconstituted' (in demographers' argot).

Generally, the point cannot be too strongly stressed that single parenthood—regarded by many Conservatives as a form of moral plague ('the most socially subversive institution of our time' according to P. Johnson)—is not a static condition, still less an immoral one. Rather, it is a stage in the life cycle which may lead in a variety of different directions, with widely various consequences. The decline in the popularity of marriage, which has helped to produce higher rates of 'illegitimacy', is itself a stage in a process of development which is taking this country in the direction not of the American model (which, as Murray rightly points out, is far more heavily influenced by the race factor than our own) but the Scandinavian. Sweden and Denmark already have illegitimacy rates twice as high as those in this country; yet the great majority of children there are born into two-parent families and civil society has survived without the dire consequences with which Murray threatens us.

Crime Rates

Crime rates, Murray's second exhibit, need not detain us long. No-one who (like the present writer) has had first-hand acquaintance with the collection of criminal statistics would dream of using them as the basis for a theory of social change. But, since Murray is quite properly interested as much in perceptions of the prevalence of violent crime as in its actual incidence, it is odd that he did not think fit to consult the British Crime Survey. The contrasts that this shows between popular anxieties and realities could perhaps be said to 'force theory to its knees', in Murray's colourful phrase—unhappily, his is the theory that ends in that uncomfortable posture.

Unemployment

On unemployment, Murray is on much firmer ground. Paradoxically, data disappear abruptly from sight at this stage in his argument—presumably because the Government's tampering with the unemployment statistics has made comparison over time virtually impossible. Despite these misconceived attempts to hold up the weather by breaking the bloody glass, however, it seems clear that the rapid growth in unemployment which began at the end of the 1970s (not 'late' in the 1970s, incidentally, when it was going down: Mr Murray is Tebbiting here) has been the single most significant factor in increasing poverty during the 1980s. It has also had a differential impact, by class, region, age, and race. Murray is absolutely right to insist on the central importance of this factor and on its potentially long lasting consequences, in terms of the experience of a whole generation of young people who were unable to obtain entry to the labour market. What he could have added—but didn't—is that much of this growth in unemployment can be directly attributed to the Government's own policies (half, at least, according to an authoritative analysis by the House of Lords Select Committee on Unemployment [1983]).

Consideration of where to go next makes up the remainder of Murray's contribution, which is mostly remarkable for its scepticism about the role of governments, present and future. In fact, given that the mass unemployment of the 1980s was fuelled by Government policies, it is logical enough to suppose that changing them (both policies and Government) is a more promising way of starting to achieve lasting reductions than statistical juggling. Since the Government currently seems determined to repeat the mistakes of the early 1980s and squeeze British industry once again within an inch of its life or beyond, with a concomitant repetition of the disastrous pattern of job losses—but this time in services as well as manufacturing—this task is rapidly becoming urgent.

Benefits

The issue of benefits is more complex. Mr Murray is to be commended for refusing to buy the nostrum being peddled by the British New Right moralists. He has no objection to providing basic support for single parents and their children through the early stages of child rearing; but persists in seeing an element of perverse incentives in providing generously beyond that point. Evidently, the cultural arguments weigh more strongly with him than the public health ones (having praised Frank Field's recent work on the underclass, Murray should now reread Field on the persistence of class differentials in mortality). Here, child benefit is vital in helping to float single parents successfully through the dependent stage when their children are young to the point when they can re-enter the labour market. Some of them already do—45 per cent of mothers with children aged 3-4, for example—despite 'overwhelming constraints in terms of lack of job opportunities, the availability of only low-paid work and the difficulties of providing childcare'.[1] Forms of assistance that would enable them to do so in larger numbers are a crucial policy priority. Labour market policies as well as benefits need to be adjusted (compare with the successful Swedish model); more support from Government, in the form of cash as well as improved quality and availability of child care services, is a legitimate national investment—as Eleanor Rathbone pointed out long before Beveridge.

'Little Platoons'

Perhaps the most interesting passage in Mr Murray's otherwise sparse list for action is the one he hardly develops at all; the notion that much of the work on breaking up (or down) the underclass (if it does indeed exist) will have to be done at the local level. Here, the centripetal tendencies of Thatcher Government policies have inflicted quite unnecessary damage on the capacity of localities to take effective initiatives. Murray calls for 'a massive dose of self-government'; fine, but where are the resources, human and financial, to come from? He airily asserts that it is easy to combine sustaining current levels of expenditure for public systems with decentralised control over them. I do not think he can have much recent acquaintance with HM Treasury, and its present attitudes towards public expenditure.

Here again, it is reversal of existing policy that supplies the logical starting point; the experiments in decentralisation of service delivery and local control which began under the banner of 'municipal socialism' in the 1980s, whose success was compromised by the Government's vendetta against local authorities, need to be re-examined and the lessons applied (and if Mr Murray believes that such measures have not yet been seriously explored he should forthwith consult the oracles—at Bristol, for example).

Elsewhere, (in *In Pursuit*),[2] Mr Murray has argued, if I have understood him correctly, for a systematic devolution of power to the 'little platoons' (one more time, that old Burkean rag). These are to be essentially voluntary associations acting independently of the state. Withdrawal by the state from service delivery will allow the individual citizen to earn his civic status by showing that he is 'pulling his own weight'. Those who do not, like single-parent families, will need 'prodding' into recognition of the need to do so. Alternatively, they should find refuge among their own kind, and allow neighbourhoods which value two-parent status to flourish without contamination.

Concealed Authoritarianism

To which I would respond: neighbourhood autonomy by all means; but not through the imposition of artificial homogeneity of values, class composition, or even race. One key difficulty with the platoon as an image is its barely concealed authoritarianism: with Burke as our patron saint, distinctions of rank and degree cannot fail to be faithfully observed. If they are not, how are essential services to be supplied to the autonomous neighbourhood: the 'innumerable servile, degrading, unseemly, unmanly, and often most unwholesome and pestiferous occupations to which by the social economy so many wretches are inevitably doomed' (Burke again)? No doubt these wretches can be bussed in from outside; but isn't that a trifle, well, South African?

Nor am I clear how far Murray would allow welfare policy to be a matter of local discretion. It is not difficult to imagine local control that leads straight back to the Poor Law—Elizabethan, that is, which had a particularly vigorous line in prodding those whose occupations or morals did not square with local values.

Democracy

The virtues of some form of local control are not in doubt: any dispute is about how it is to be exercised—who is accountable to whom for which activities. There is an implicit pessimism (cynicism, even) about the form that Murray advocates and the limits he sets, as when he comments—ironically, I assume—that poverty 'needn't bother us as long as it stays in its own part of town'. At root, this pessimism springs from scepticism about democracy and the possibility of articulating choices through disinterested debate within a democratic system. In their pessimism, Marxist and Conservative once again join hands. To them, democracy merely provides the screen behind which the executive committee of the bourgeoisie or the self-aggrandizement of the bureau maximiser can function unchallenged. Personally, I find it dispiriting that an American, of all people, should be preaching the virtues of a static form of society composed of neatly docketed and differentiated small units from which the dangerous classes have been carefully excluded.

But perhaps we can take some comfort from Mr Murray's recognition that 'Britain in 1989 has resources that make predicting the course of the underclass on the basis of the US experience very dicey'. As in the late 1960s, the clouds may roll over without shedding their rain. Even if some drops do fall, it may be best not to rush to embark in Mr Murray's Ark quite yet—at least, until we know how soundly constructed it really is.

Notes

1 Lewis, J., 'Lone Parent Families', *Journal of Social Policy*, October 1989.

2 Murray, C., *In Pursuit of Happiness*, New York: Simon and Schuster, 1988.

Rejoinder

Charles Murray

Introduction

I picked up the four responses to *The Emerging British Underclass* gloomily, having been through this sort of thing before and not looking forward to doing it again. But, as I read, I became progressively more cheerful, finally laughing out loud when Nicholas Deakin parenthetically admonished me for 'Tebbiting' because I argued that British unemployment had grown in the 'late' 1970s rather than at the 'end'. In the US, where this sort of thrust and parry is generally conducted with maces, no-one could have raised a quibble—but a well-taken quibble—so gracefully and goodnaturedly. In any case, let me begin by saying that I thought the papers by Field, Brown, and Deakin, do not really require a rejoinder for the best of reasons: their commentaries fairly and resourcefully defend a point of view that I attacked; I am, nevertheless, unpersuaded, for reasons that I think were already stated adequately in my original article; and I will be satisfied if the reader simply goes back and takes another look at *The Emerging British Underclass* side-by-side with their observations. My own comments about these comment-aries are less in the form of rebuttal than an attempt to minimise confusion and maximise authentic disagreement.

I should add that I enjoyed Professor Walker's paper as well, albeit in another way. It is the kind of undiluted statement of Left dogma on this topic that is fast disappearing—a sort of modern Rousseauism in which the noble savage is replaced by the noble poor person —written, as the rules apparently require, so as to convey that the Left's intellectual adversaries are not only wrong, but incompetent; not only incompetent, but sinister. And so to the main points at issue.

Is there a Legitimate Behavioural Distinction to be drawn among Classes of Poor People?

If I had to pick out the one point on which confusion is most intertwined with real disagreement, it would be the question of whether an underclass exists at all. Even when the word is admitted, people use it differently. Frank Field's usage is quite different from mine, for example, defining the underclass by condition (the very frail elderly pensioner, the long-term unemployed, and the poor single parent), whereas I defined it by behaviour—some long-term unemployed are members of the underclass, others, like the long-term unemployed family in Birkenhead that I cited in *The Emerging British Underclass,* are unequivocally not. Some single mothers qualify; others do not, and so forth. I would exclude frail, elderly pensioners altogether—the problem represented by the frail, elderly pensioner with too little money is that he has too little money, and the problem is solved (more or less) by giving him more money. Questions of moral hazard arise only at second or third hand. Questions of present behaviour arise not at all.

When I use the term 'underclass' I am indeed focusing on a certain type of poor person defined not by his condition, e.g. long-term unemployed, but by his deplorable behaviour in response to that condition, e.g. unwilling to take the jobs that are available to him. The question remains, however, whether there is an empirical reality behind my statements about deplorable behaviour. Walker thinks not, emphatically. Science has conducted surveys, and science has proved that I am deluded —there is, in his words, an 'overwhelming weight of scientific evidence against' the notion of an underclass. And, the nature of this overwhelming weight of evidence? He begins by citing proof that 'At least half of the children born into a disadvantaged home do not repeat the pattern of disadvantage in the next generation'. Then he cited evidence that among a representative sample of young people, many (he did not say what proportion, but presumably it was large) continued to 'search for employment in the face of repeated failure and disappointment'. All of this makes sense to me. In fact, I am a little surprised that the proportion who 'repeat the pattern of disadvantage' is as high as 50 per cent. As for unemployment, I am already on record in *The Emerging British Underclass,* when I wrote that 'I am not suggesting that a third or a quarter or even a fifth of lower-class young people are indifferent to work', for example.

This points to a larger misreading of *The Emerging British Underclass* which, though common among my critics, remains mystifying to me. How can people read my extensive descriptions of causation, all of which focus on the ways in which members are responding sensibly (at least in the short term) to policies that have been put in place around them, and then cite surveys regarding a 'culture of poverty' to refute me? The burden of my argument is that members of the underclass are *not* sunk in a cultural bog; that all people who are poor do *not* repeat the cycle of disadvantage, whereas others do, and the interesting question is why the latter group (which has existed from time immemorial) has existed in such different proportions in different societies at different times, and in the industrialised west seems, in recent years, to have grown rapidly. I am arguing for disaggregation of the data about poor people. Which segments of the poor population 'repeat the pattern of disadvantage'? Are they randomly scattered throughout people below a certain income level, or are there common elements among them? Which segments of the unemployed search diligently for work and which do not? I am arguing that there is an ecology to poverty. Cross-sectional surveys of poor people or of the unemployed that detail population parameters are useless in either confirming or disconfirming this hypothesis.

Observational Evidence

If one wants to talk about evidence on this topic, the richest and most informative evidence is in the form of observation, and the library is large. Let me make a statement as sweeping as Walker's about overwhelming evidence: regarding the United States, I know of no scientific observational study of poor communities in America, beginning with W.E.B. DuBois' pioneering *The Philadelphia Negro* in 1890, that does *not* describe class difference within low-income populations that conform to my distinction between poor people and the underclass. There is an interesting distinction here worth pondering: those who say that there is no underclass tend to rely on studies in which scholars go into poor neighbourhoods for a few hours at a time with clipboards and multiple-choice questionnaires. Those who say there is an underclass tend to rely on studies in which scholars live in poor communities, and get their information from long conversations conducted over weeks and months with the people who live there.

Because I am not nearly as familiar with the literature in Britain, I will content myself with this additional sweeping observation, and readers may judge from their own experience whether it is true: The people who deal most intimately with poor communities in their daily lives use the same distinction among poor people that I use. The managers of council estates, policemen in poor neighbourhoods, social workers, nurses, and physicians, may or may not bridle at the term 'underclass', but if the topic of conversation is not whether this American reactionary is right, but rather a leisurely discussion of how these people go about their work and what life is like in the communities where they work, the distinction between the good folks and the underclass shines through after the first five minutes.

However we need not continue this debate endlessly. Regarding unemployment, at least, there is a simple, fairly conclusive test that I suggested in *The Emerging British Underclass* and hereby propose once more. Find a philanthropist or government agency that will fund a few hundred full-time, low-skill jobs at decent pay. Get to a poor urban neighbourhood convenient to the job site. Seek out a representative sample of unemployed young men, and ask each if he wants a job. Almost all will say yes, probably accompanied by many harsh words about Mrs Thatcher. Then offer them the jobs you have available. Record their behavioural response to this opportunity. Count who does what. Follow those who actually take the jobs for the next year. And you will have your answer, or much of the answer, to the size and nature of the underclass among unemployed young men.

What is the Comparative Role of Individual Behaviour and Structural Causes?

Am I blaming the victim, as Walker insists? In one sense, obviously not. I am blaming governments for wrong-headed policies that seduce people into behaving in ways that seem sensible in the short term but are disastrous in the long term.

In a second sense, blame does not come into the argument at all. I am simply observing that a behaviour exists and that it has pernicious social consequences. If my critics were to prove to me irrefutably that the people who are behaving in these deplorable ways are in no way free agents, it would not change anything in my analysis.

In a third sense, I am using the concept of blame as a useful fiction. America's Jesse Jackson puts it well when he tells black teenagers that 'It may not be your fault if someone knocks you down, but it's your fault if you don't get up'. I put it somewhat differently in *Losing Ground* when I wrote that even if it is true that a poor young person is not responsible for the condition in which he finds himself, the worst thing one can do is try to persuade him of that.

The Importance of Blame

In a fourth sense, I want to reintroduce the notion of blame, and sharply reduce our readiness to call people 'victims', for this compelling reason: British intellectuals and (despite Mrs Thatcher) British social policy remain overwhelmingly on the side of the poor youngster who fails in school, gets in trouble with the law, does not hold a job, or has a child without being able to care for it. Youths who do any of these things will find no shortage of social workers and academics prepared to make excuses to try to shield them from the consequences of their behaviour. I am more concerned about the poor youngster who is studying hard, obeying the law, working hard, and taking care not to have a baby. Forget (for a moment) about the ethics and just deserts of this situation and consider hard-headedly that Britain badly needs lots of young people to behave in these desirable ways, and the straightforward way to achieve that end is in a context where such behaviour is praised and rewarded. The difficulty is that, by taking away responsibility—by saying, 'Because the system is to blame, it's not your fault that...'—society also takes away the credit that is an essential part of the reward structure that fosters social and economic mobility. It is impossible to tell someone persuasively that he did well regarding one form of behaviour unless he may also be told that he did badly regarding another. Blame is essential if one is to praise.

Moral Judgement

In a fifth sense—yes, Professor Walker, your deepest fears are justified—I do want to reintroduce the notion of genuine blame in a moral sense. The standard to which I hold myself, and which I advocate for other commentators on social policy, is: do not apply a different moral standard to strangers—including poor strangers—from the standard which applies to the people one knows and loves. I bring moral judgement to bear on the behaviour of my children, wife, friends—and myself. If I say of strangers that they are exempt, why? Because they are less intelligent? My own childhood environment left something to be desired. So did the environment that my children grew up in. The environment that my parents grew up in was plain awful. We are all indeed brothers and sisters under the skin, and we deserve the respect of being held accountable.

To bring moral judgement to bear does not mean Cromwellian severity. If one of my daughters, single and without the resources to raise a child on her own, comes home pregnant, I am not obliged to throw her out of the house. But I will think what she did is wrong. Not just a mistake, nor just a miscalculation, but wrong. I will tell her so. I will love her, help her, and think hard thoughts about the male who collaborated, and find fault with myself as a father... but none of that will change the underlying reaction that is in my view essential for the sustenance of a civilized society. I will blame her. If it were somehow possible for government institutions to do the same thing—to love, help, but also to hold people morally responsible for their behaviour—then I would have far fewer objections to social programmes, for I think they would do far more good and far less harm. Unfortunately, we do not know how to make governmental institutions act that way.

Is Illegitimacy really such a Terrible Problem?

Joan Brown's handling of the data regarding lone births, marriages, and cohabitation, adds significantly to my description in *The Emerging British Underclass;* and the contrasts between the British and American situation are well-taken. Regarding Britain, however, I am not sure, that the data she cites portray a picture much different from the one I portrayed.

The case she makes, with general agreement from Walker and Deakin, goes roughly like this: yes, births to single women have increased as a proportion of live births, but this does not necessarily mean that the children of these marriages are growing up without fathers. Cohabitation has increased dramatically. Moreover, single women who have babies typically get married within a few years of birth. In contrast to the US experience, only about a quarter of unmarried mothers remain on benefit for as long as five years. Taking these factors together, then, my fears about communities without fathers are overdrawn.

First, a technical addendum to Brown's data: I did not use the Ermisch data that Brown and Walker both cite for a reason to which Brown alludes but which deserves more emphasis: Ermisch's data were based on a representative sample of women aged 16-59 as of 1980, which means that he was examining marital dynamics for women who came to childbearing age beginning in the mid-1930s. The massive change in the proportion of children born to single women began in the late 1970s. This raises two difficulties. The first is a problem of truncation in the data: the youngest women in his sample, whose experience was closest in time to the era in which the illegitimacy problem increased, had 'had time' to experience no more than a few years of lone parenthood before data collection came to an end. If changes in behaviour were occurring regarding remarriage, Ermisch's data could not have revealed it.

The second difficulty is the life experience of a young woman who had a child without a husband in the 1960s and early 1970s is likely to be an uncertain guide in assessing what is going on with such women in the 1980s; the experience of those who had a child without a husband in the 1930s, 1940s and 1950s, is likely to be positively misleading. Nothing in Ermisch's article addresses these potential cohort effects. Perhaps Brown is right in predicting that more recent data will not reveal much change in the average number of years between the birth of a child and eventual marriage (to someone, not necessarily the father). But, based on her own discussion of the number of single mothers who are on benefit for more than five years (probably a good proxy measure for failure to marry), something is happening that suggests changes. It would be illuminating to plot that proportion of long-term recipients from 1970 through 1987 and see what the curve looks like—but I must leave that to Brown, since I do not have that data series presently available to me.

Illegitimacy and Socio-Economic Status

The main point, however, is that the data Brown reviews (even disregarding the technical issues) are consistent with the portrait I drew in *The Emerging British Underclass*. This is most easily seen by trying to translate the statistics on marriage into a playgroup of a dozen children living on a council estate. As I indicated in *The Emerging British Underclass*, illegitimacy in England (as in the US) has a strong inverse statistical association with socio-economic status. Municipalities with large proportions of lower-class households have much higher illegitimacy ratios than municipalities with small proportions of lower-class households; and lower-class neighbourhoods within a given municipality have higher rates than the municipal average. With an overall national ratio of 25 per cent, the typical ratio for a poor municipality is 35-45 per cent, and the ratio within council estates in those communities is by mathematical necessity (given the known socio-economic link) considerably higher.

Applying these considerations to the dozen playmates, what is the likely profile of their family histories and current family situations?

Trying to estimate the specific number of children in the various situations would take me far afield—the calculations become statistically quite complex, involving expected values and distributional probabilities for a complicated set of permutations. But even taking the unadorned illegitimacy ratios in poor communities, the numbers Brown cites regarding cohabitation, adding in the additional effects of divorces, and making a rough mental estimate, should make the point plain: only a minority of the dozen children are likely to be living in two-parent families, and almost all will have experienced spells of living in a two-parent family and spells of living with a single parent. Now, add into this picture the flesh and bones of what the parents, the marriages, and the parenting are like.

Here, I think, *The Emerging British Underclass* needed another paragraph elaborating on the experience of one of my informants, the unemployed family in Birkenhead. This exceptionally articulate and thoughtful couple are no fans of Mrs Thatcher's; on the contrary, they are staunch Labourites who hold no brief for my Whig solutions. But the story they told, I cannot stress sufficiently, must be heard by people who are trying to interpret the numbers. Yes, some of the mothers in their neighbourhood around them were cohabiting in a relationship, but this was seldom a plus, more often a negative. The cohabitations were not those of loving parents, but more often of stormy, highly unstable relationships. In cases where remarriage had occurred, there were few kindly stepfathers and too many who saw the kids they had inherited as a nuisance. Adding up the women who had never married or cohabited, plus those who were between boyfriends, plus those who were between husbands, plus those who had abusive husbands, and there were very few families.

I will be happy to see the same exercise performed for a playgroup in a middle-class neighbourhood, but readers who are parents will not need to wait for that. All they have to do is think about the playgroup to which their children belong. Yes, there are likely to be some in the group whose parents were divorced. But (I am asserting: do the counting for yourself), the chances are that at any one time a solid majority of the children are living in two-parent households, several of them (probably a majority) are living in households in which there has never been a divorce, and hardly any of the children are living with a mother who has had three, four, or more, live-in partners. Even in a world of high divorce rates in which the breakdown of the family is lamented, the familial world of middle-class and upper-class children is importantly different from the world of the underclass.

Is Cohabitation Equivalent to Marriage?

One final question before leaving this topic, and it is not rhetorical: Why are the British, or at least the British represented among these commentators, so ready to assume that cohabitation means a stable relationship that is more or less equivalent (for purposes of rearing young children) to marriage? I know of nothing in the US experience with cohabitation to suggest confidence. On the contrary, cohabitation often seems as likely to be a minus for the child as a plus. Are there good data on this topic that I do not know about? Or is it just not a done thing in British intellectual circles to think that marriage is fundamentally different from living together?

In this regard, I was struck by the remark by both Walker and Deakin that parts of Scandinavia have illegitimacy rates twice as high as those in Britain and yet 'civil society has survived without the dire consequences with which Murray threatens us' (Deakin, p. 76) and 'as far as I know, [Denmark] is not on the brink of disaster' (Walker, p. 70). Reading these comments, I once again had the sense of being in a time warp that stayed with me throughout my conversations with the British while I was researching *The Emerging British Underclass*. As recently as six years ago, when *Losing Ground* was first published, I was constantly responding to praise of Sweden and Denmark, which were held up as models of the welfare state. I almost never hear such statements any more, because the American champions of the Scandinavian model have lately been backpedalling. 'Brink of disaster' is still too strong a term to describe the situation facing Sweden and Denmark, but their problems have been multiplying, and embedded within those problems are ones not nearly as simple as a rise in unemployment, but ones that arise from the difficulties of trying to sustain a society and a culture without the traditional family to rely upon. The jury is still out, but on the dire consequences of illegitimacy rates at 50 per cent, I would offer Messrs. Walker and Deakin a traditional American challenge: want to bet?

Bits and Pieces

Before proceeding to the final large question, two points deserve brief mention: regarding Nicholas Deakin's paragraph about crime, he is too elliptical for me to follow. Does the British Crime Survey that I should have consulted reveal that popular anxieties about crime are greater than the reality warrants? Or is the anxiety less than the reality warrants? In either case, I cannot imagine what he means when he argues that it contradicts anything in my argument. Popular anxieties about crime are wholly irrelevant. My point is that, even after worrying about the problems with the collection of criminal statistics, the changes in violent crime rates in England bespeak a fundamental change in behaviour; that there is reason to think this is not equally a problem in rich communities and poor communities; and that this pertains to the organisation of such communities and the quality of life within them. If Deakin thinks that violent crime has not really risen in England, more or less in the steepening curve that I described, then he should say so. When he says, instead, merely that crime rates 'need not detain us long' and alludes airily to the difficulties of interpreting them, I think that Deakin is perhaps... Tebbiting.

Regarding Frank Field's comment about the distinctive nature of the American underclass, as deriving from the black sharecropper experience in the south: obviously, the British and American situations are different because of the racial experience that blights America's history, and Nick Lemann's work on the relationship of this history to the underclass is provocative and useful. I expected major differences between the underclass in America (mostly black) with the underclass in Britain (mostly white) because of these very different contexts. I was surprised, therefore, to discover how minor the differences were. Life in Birkenhead and Easterhouse was described to me in terms that sounded almost exactly like descriptions of life in South Chicago and East Harlem, the major distinction being that the British underclass is still much less violent than the American underclass. Overall, my experience in Britain tended to reinforce the conclusion that the etiology of the underclass derives more from policy than from cultural context.

What is to be Done?

Perhaps the most common reaction to *The Emerging British Underclass* from readers at large is that I neglected or gave too little space to policy recommendations. I did so for a reason that I will state explicitly here.

In my views about policy, I find that I have become (somewhat to my surprise, for I am not temperamentally so) an authentic radical. I am persuaded that a limited central government is not only feasible in the late 20th-century, but would be a far better way to run modern society than the methods we now use. By 'limited central government', I mean a Jeffersonian system in which the central government protects the sanctity of voluntary mutual agreements (including the enforcement of contracts through civil law), and protection of people from physical coercion, and fraud by others (whether they be foreign invaders or the fellow next door). I am not a purist—I think there are other public goods, classically defined, that warrant central government funding and intervention—but I am, by any contemporary understanding, nonetheless, outside the mainstream of politics. Even the more moderate reforms that I am prepared to recommend on grounds that they will make matters better are pretty radical (educational vouchers in place of state education, for example). I do not have in my head that set of policy recommendations that every proper writer about social policy is supposed to have, a list of incremental, politically practicable reforms. I can concoct none that I can persuade myself would do any good.

At the same time, I think my analysis of social problems needs to be considered seriously. Hence the quandary: for me to expand on my policy prescriptions is to give large numbers of readers too easy an excuse for ignoring my analysis of the problem, on grounds that I am obviously a nut. So I do not say much about policy.

But the nature of my views nevertheless creates an abyss separating me from the four commentators on this topic. Professor Walker carries the egalitarian banner without visible second thoughts, leaving me shaking my head that anyone could still be so benighted, just as he doubtless regards me. Joan Brown takes a pragmatic stance, but in doing so presents an underlying dilemma: 'The reality is that, practically and ethically, we have to start from where we are', she writes. 'That means we have to be prepared to put effort and resources into programmes aimed at strengthening the two-parent family... But we must also seek to strengthen the ability of one-parent families to offer their children a sound family life, for as long as they hold that status' (p. 65).

It cannot be done, in my view. Policies that make the one-parent situation tolerable produce more one-parent families, for the constellation of reasons I discussed in *The Emerging British Underclass*. The strength of the two-parent family is inescapably undermined by those policies. The difficulty in pursuing this line of reasoning, however, is underlined by Brown's remark that 'I have never seen the social morality of storming the barricades over the bodies of living children' (p. 64). In making social policy, we see the needs and the pains of the living children before us, and the imperative to do something for them is overwhelming. Using the Government as the instrument is irresistibly encompassing, efficient, and quick. What we cannot see, and refuse even to contemplate in the mind's eye, is the ways in which these same policies, indirectly but just as concretely, create children with needs and with pain. What someday we must acknowledge is that these policies in the end create more pain than they alleviate.

Stop Thinking as Engineers

When it comes to policy, Frank Field is the iconoclast and the optimist, moving far afield from Labour doctrine in order to engineer schemes for dealing with single-parent families and integrating young men back into the labour force. I admire the energy and the imagination that go into those schemes, but I react with the perspective of a person who for 12 years made his living by evaluating such programmes on contract to various departments of the US federal government. There are stacks of such evaluations—of employment programmes, programmes for single parents and every other conceivable kind of programme, some of them as imaginative and energetic as Field's, tried in the States from 1964 to 1980. The evaluations were mostly written by sympathetic observers who tried their best to tease out whatever evidence of success they could find. Nonetheless, they chronicle virtually unrelieved failure. The reason the programmes failed is not because they were inadequately funded nor because the people who ran them were inadequately talented or motivated. Rather, complex social programmes intended to change human behaviour tend not to work out the way they were planned. We are not going to make progress until we stop thinking as engineers, and instead return to think of society as an organism that must be allowed to return to health.

That 'old Burkean rag' yet once again, Professor Deakin says. Actually, Deakin seems drawn himself to local autonomy, but he worries about the ways in which little platoons can become small tyrannies. When he writes 'neighbourhood autonomy by all means, but not through the imposition of artificial homogeneity of values, class composition, or even race' (p. 79), I agree wholeheartedly. I suspect, however, that we have different conceptions of how 'artificial homogeneity' comes about.

Small Tyrannies

But let me address the problem of small tyrannies more directly. My proposition is that humans acting in a private capacity *if restrained from the use of force* have a remarkably good history. To test this, I would ask you to pick your favourite image of people acting oppressively. Now ask: under what conditions were these villains able to do these bad things for a long time without the connivance of the state, without special laws or privileges being granted on their behalf, and without being allowed by the state (if only turning a blind eye) to use physical coercion? I suggest that the longer we consider each specific instance that comes to mind, the more plausible we find this rule of thumb: it is really very difficult for people—including large associations of people and huge corporations—to do anything very bad, for very long, when they are not buttressed by the threat of physical coercion. Private oppression deprived of access to force withers away rather rapidly.

Deakin then wonders how the 'degrading' but essential work is to be done in my autonomous neighbourhoods, wondering if the 'wretches' will have to be imported unless the community resorts to authoritarian methods. He finds it 'dispiriting that an American, of all people, should be preaching the virtues of a static form of society composed of neatly docketed and differentiated small units from which the dangerous classes have been carefully excluded' (p. 79). Perhaps we have arrived at last to that difference between Americans and the British which I tried to keep in mind as I wrote *The Emerging British Underclass,* for I cannot imagine what kind of communities Professor Deakin has experienced that lead him to those extraordinary assumptions about how communities work.

Autonomous Communities

When I think of autonomous communities, I think of the mid-western town where I grew up. I remember school rooms where the children of corporate executives were best buddies with the children of assembly line workers, church congregations in which every social class was mixed, children growing up thinking that being a garbage collector or a cleaning lady or a janitor was respectable, because the first lesson we were taught was that the only degrading kind of work was no work. I also remember children leaving that community—my wife and I were two of them—into every sort of profession, every corner of the country and the world, in a veritable riot of social and economic mobility. This is 'static'? This is 'neatly docketed'? This is exclusionary and authoritarian? Perhaps I lived in an idyllic community and am thereby misled. But we must consider also the possibility that this is the way that communities of free people tend to function, and that to achieve a society of such communities requires not that governments engineer them, but that governments get out of the way.

PART 2

Underclass: The Crisis Deepens

Foreword (1994 edition)

When *The Sunday Times* brought Charles Murray to Britain in 1989, he described himself as a visitor from a plague area who had come to see whether the disease was spreading. His conclusion was:

> Britain does have an underclass, still largely out of sight and still smaller than the one in the United States. But it is growing rapidly. Within the next decade, it will probably become as large (proportionately) as the United States' underclass. It could easily become larger.

Five years on, how well has Charles Murray's argument fared?

Initially published in *The Sunday Times' Magazine* in November 1989, Dr Murray's essay was re-published by the IEA in early 1990 along with commentaries by three academics and the Labour MP, Frank Field. The academics treated the argument with disdain, contending that Murray's evidence did not support his main thesis. He based his claim on three measures: illegitimacy, violent crime and drop-out from the labour force. The original article was based on data for 1987; the 1994 update is based on figures for 1992.

Between 1987 and 1992 property crime in England and Wales increased by 42 per cent, while America's remained unchanged. By 1992 the risk of being burgled in England and Wales was more than double that in the US. The violent crime rate increased by 40 per cent, so that the rate in England and Wales in 1992 was the same as the United States' in 1985. On illegitimacy Murray's predictions have also been confirmed. In 1987 23 per cent of births in England and Wales occurred outside marriage. In 1992 the figure was 31 per cent. Murray's concern about dropping out of the labour force is not captured by unemployment or economic activity statistics and in his 1994 article Murray does not press home his analysis of labour-force dropout, conceding that other factors may be influential. He concentrates instead on the problem he considers to be the root cause of the rising underclass, the breakdown of the family.

In focusing on the family Charles Murray follows a long line of classical liberals, from Adam Smith onwards, who understood the importance of solid family life in equipping children with the personal skills and moral dispositions fundamental to the free way of life we have enjoyed in the West. In *The Fatal Conceit* Hayek stresses the importance of religions in protecting the two fundamental pillars of freedom: the family and property. Not all religions have done so, but according to Hayek, the only religious movements to flourish have been those which supported both property and the family.[1]

Adam Smith believed that the law should for the most part prohibit injury rather than lay specific obligations on people, but he thought the family was one of the exceptions: 'The laws of all civilized nations', he says, 'oblige parents to maintain their children, and children to maintain their parents'.[2] He also opposed easy divorce. If it was too easy, he argued, it tended to undermine trust between the couple because both were 'continually in fear of being dismissed by the other party'. He accepted that divorce law could be too strict, but thought it better that the knot was 'too strait' than too loose.[3] And in keeping with his view that family life depends on regular close contact, Adam Smith urged parents not to send their children away to boarding schools because, by living at home, 'Respect for you must always impose a very useful restraint upon their conduct; and respect for them may frequently impose no useless restraint upon your own'.[4]

To add to its value for teachers in schools and universities who wish to present students with both sides of the argument in a single book, Dr Murray's paper is accompanied by four commentaries: one by the distinguished newspaper columnist, Melanie Phillips; a second by the Director of the National Council for One-Parent Families, Sue Slipman; and two by academics, Professor Pete Alcock of Sheffield Hallam University and Professor Miriam David of South Bank University.

Dr David G. Green

Notes

1   Hayek, F.A., *The Fatal Conceit*, London: Routledge, 1988, p. 137.

2   Smith, A., *The Theory of Moral Sentiments*, Indianapolis, Liberty Fund, 1969, p. 159.

3   Smith, A., *Lectures on Jurisprudence*, Indianapolis: Liberty Fund, 1978, p. 160.

4   Smith, *The Theory of Moral Sentiments*, p. 364.

U nderclass: The Crisis Deepens

Charles Murray

Introduction

Five years ago, *The Sunday Times* brought me to England to ask whether this country was developing an American-style underclass. It looked to me then as if England was replaying the American scenario, and I said so in a long article published first in *The Sunday Times' Magazine* and subsequently in an expanded form in *The Emerging British Underclass*, published by the IEA Health and Welfare Unit. In the autumn of 1993, *The Sunday Times* brought me back to England to see how things had changed since 1989, and the result was a two-part article published in May 1994. Those articles were a condensed version of a longer discussion that is presented here in full.

Symptoms of the British Underclass, 1987 and 1992

When trying to estimate what's happening to the underclass, I focus on three symptoms: crime, illegitimacy, and economic inactivity among working-aged men. Five years ago, I was looking at data for 1987; this year, I am looking at data for 1992.

Crime: When I last visited, the property crime rate in England and Wales (which I will shorten to 'England' from now on) was already slightly higher than America's. Since then English property crime has jumped another 42 per cent, while America's is unchanged. The net result is that property crime is now much more widespread in England than in the United States—for example, the risk of being burgled in England is more than twice that in the United States. The more important marker of an underclass is probably violent crime, indicating as it does a more profound detachment from the standards of a civil society. Five years ago, the public was upset about a violent crime rate that had reached 397 per 100,000 people. That number has gone up 40 per cent since then. Given the reputation of the United States when it comes to violent crime, perhaps this statistic will give you pause: the violent crime rate in England is the same as it was in the United States in 1985. The good news, such as it is, is that murder is still much rarer in England than in America.

Illegitimacy: I will have much more to say on this topic. Briefly, the staggering increases of the preceding decade continued throughout the next five years. In 1987, 23.3 per cent of English births occurred outside marriage; by 1992, the figure had grown to 31.2 per cent. If England continues the trend it has followed since 1980—you passed the 33 per cent mark this year—half of all births will be out of wedlock by 2003.

Impossible? American blacks were at the same figure in 1966 that the English were in 1990—30 per cent. Their illegitimacy ratio did not level off after reaching 30 per cent; it accelerated, passing the 50 per cent mark in just ten more years. The English won't behave like American blacks? It took American blacks 11 years to go from 20 per cent to 30 per cent of births out of wedlock. It took the English only six years to make the same trip.

Economic Inactivity: In the 1981 census, 11.3 per cent of working-aged men (16-64) in the labour force were unemployed, (defined as men available for work), while 9.6 per cent of working-aged men were economically inactive altogether (including those who do not consider themselves available for work).[1] In the 1991 census, unemployment of the working-aged was almost identical (11.0 per cent), but the percentage of working-aged men who were economically inactive had increased by more than a third to 13.3 per cent.[2] It is difficult to know what to make of this without much more information, but the trend is in a worrisome direction.

The other big difference between 1989 and today has nothing to do with statistics, but with the public mood. Five years ago, the idea that England was developing an underclass attracted harsh scepticism. I had failed to make my case with 'scientific evidence', as one academic critic put it. My thesis was not only 'misleading', but 'perhaps wilfully so'.[3] By autumn 1993 when I visited, the idea of an underclass got a more sympathetic hearing. As I talked to people around the country, there still existed an obvious split between the intellectuals and the man in the street, with many intellectuals continuing to dismiss problems of crime and single parenthood as nothing more than a 'moral panic'. But John Redwood's Cardiff speech in July had brought the debate about illegitimacy into the open. The day I arrived in London in September, I turned on the television to find *Panorama* running an unsympathetic portrait of single mothers and the BBC's *Breakfast News* beginning a five-day examination of British crime that, unlike five years ago, did not reflexively assume that the public was getting excited over nothing. Among intellectuals and politicians alike, the larger meanings of crime and illegitimacy were being taken more seriously.

But where does this leave us? An emerging consensus agrees that something resembling an underclass is growing, but there is still no consensus about what ought to be done, nor any clear sense of priorities. People may be openly worrying about problems they didn't use to worry about, but it is hard to find anyone in the Cabinet or the Opposition who has a programme that will plausibly do much to change anything. Crime is bad, of course, but sending people to prison isn't working, is it? The costs of the benefit system are too high, but cutting benefits would drive women and their children into destitution, wouldn't it? And if there aren't any jobs available, then of course nobody can blame men for eventually getting discouraged and dropping out of the labour force.

In this discussion, I will present a radical position. It focuses on recent changes in the English family. The path will be long and winding, but it comes down to three themes:

First, the transforming nature of the change in the English family has to be faced squarely. Too much of the debate still proceeds from a foggy impression that people have always been complaining about the breakdown of the family, and that the events of the last fifteen years are much like other cycles in English history that England has survived nicely. We may debate endlessly about what the consequences of the changes in the family will be, but the changes (which are continuing as I write) have been so vast and so unprecedented that they may soberly be described as revolutionary. That much, I will contend, has to be the common starting point for talking about everything else in the debate over the family.

Second, I want to broach a new way of interpreting trends. In trying to make sense of what is going on with the English family, I talked to many experts from disparate viewpoints, but all of them seemed in broad agreement that the trends pervade English society from top to bottom and that those at the top actually have more to answer for than those at the bottom. I will enter a dissent, arguing that the family in the dominant economic class—call it the upper middle-class—is in better shape than most people think, and is likely to get better. Meanwhile, deterioration is likely to continue in the lower classes. My thesis is that English society is likely to break into a new class system, drastically unlike the old and much more hostile to free institutions.

Third, I want to prompt consideration of a new range of responses. The policy options that are currently under consideration in England seem almost perversely irrelevant to the nature of the problem. I will contend that solutions are not going to be found in minor fiddling with the benefit system. A top-to-bottom overhaul of the benefit system is necessary, and it must start with answers to an elemental question: What is it worth to restore the two-parent family as the norm throughout English society?

To begin, I will lay some groundwork on four basics about the family: illegitimacy, divorce, cohabitation, and their current relationship to social class. None of the material is particularly controversial—most of the numbers come straight from the census, and are straightforward—but perspective is vital if one is to see how authentically revolutionary the changes have been. Then, I will turn to the likely effects of the revolution on English society. Finally comes the question of what, if anything, can be done.

The Statistical State of the British Family

Illegitimacy

The basics about illegitimacy are available for England as few other countries, going all the way back to the last years of Henry VIII. Figure 1 (p. 128) shows the percentage of children born outside of marriage (in five-year averages) first based on parish ecclesiastical records and, since the 1840s, on the civil register.

As Henry VIII was ending his reign, the ecclesiastical records of the time recorded 4.4 per cent of births to single women. When Elizabeth II took the throne 500 years later, an almost identical 4.8 per cent of births were to single women. In between, the percentage dipped to its all-time low under Cromwell (no surprise there) and hits its all-time high at the end of World War II (no surprise there either), and otherwise moved within a very narrow range. Up until the middle of this century, about 95 per cent of English and Welsh children had been born to married parents for at least 500 years, give or take a few percentage points.

The numbers began moving up in the last half of the 1950s and continued to climb during the 1960s and first half of the 1970s—rapidly by Britain's historic standards, but still amounting to only a few tenths of a percentage point per year. As late as 1976, only 9.2 per cent of English children were born out of wedlock. Then, for reasons we will consider subsequently, illegitimacy in England exploded. The trendline tilted sharply upward in 1977-80, and accelerated again the early 1980s. In the last few years, the rate of increase has slackened, but only fractionally.

Even if the illegitimacy were to stop right where it is (which it won't), the extent of the change has been phenomenal. It is easy to become inured to numbers, so perhaps this is a good time to pause for a moment to contemplate that figure of 31.2 per cent. Almost one of every three children born to English parents is being born outside of marriage. You do not have to be a traditionalist to acknowledge that this is an astonishing development.

Falling Marriage, Booming Divorce

In the complicated world of causation in the social statistics, the story for divorce is about as simple as it gets. In 1969, the House of Commons passed the Divorce Reform Act, replacing the old, strict requirements for divorce with an easily demonstrated state of 'irretrievable breakdown of the marriage'. Divorce became much easier as of 1 January 1971, when the Act went into effect, and the effects of this major change became immediately apparent, see Figure 2, (p. 128).

Divorce petitions doubled in the first year that the Act was in effect, continued to rise, then more or less stabilised in the late 1970s at an annual rate, after adjusting for population change, of about three times the level preceding the Act.

The figure also shows the line for first marriages—for both parties—which chose the same moment in history to begin to plunge. The two phenomena are not formally connected in any way (the marriage line in the graph is limited to first marriages, thereby excluding the boom in remarriage caused by the increase in divorce). Why should marriages have chosen the same moment in history to drop? Fully exploring the reasons would take us far afield, but a simple answer probably has a lot of truth to it: When divorce becomes much easier, marriage becomes less meaningful, and then less valued.

I chose to use the raw numbers instead of rates-per-1,000 of the population, and to use first marriages rather than all marriages, to make a point. In the life of a community, the marriage of two young people has historically been not only the landmark rite of passage for the two people involved, but also an affirmation of the continuing vitality of the community; a joyous event; a celebration. The day that an impending divorce becomes known has historically been a moment not only of sadness for the two people involved, but an event that spreads a frisson of apprehension among friends and neighbours. A divorce is a sign of things falling apart; an event calling for commiseration and much concerned whispering. As recently as the late 1960s, England was a place where the events of vitality and celebration outnumbered the events of things-falling-apart and sadness by six to one. As of the early 1990s, they were about evenly split.

Cohabitation

This brings us to a more benign way of looking at changes in the family. Joint registration of children born out of wedlock has risen. Cohabitation has risen. Often, people marry after cohabiting. Taken together, these trends should quiet at least some of the alarm about the rise in illegitimacy. England doesn't really have rising illegitimacy, by this logic, but rising cohabitation.

Statistics from 1991 show that 74 per cent of births outside marriage were jointly registered. This figure has been rising steadily since the late 1960s, when only about 40 per cent of illegitimate births were jointly registered. Of the births that are jointly registered, about 70 per cent are to parents who show the same address, a proportion that has remained steady for the last decade.

Putting these two figures together, about 55 per cent of all children born out of wedlock have parents living at the same address —cohabiting. Thanks to two recent studies funded by the Joseph Rowntree Foundation, we have a much better sense of what these figures mean. One of those studies, by Susan McRae, tells us about the situation four and a half years after birth: 46 per cent were still cohabiting with someone (not necessarily the same person), 31 per cent were married (not necessarily to the father of the child), and 23 per cent were living alone.[4] In another study of cohabitation by Kathleen Kiernan and Valerie Estaugh, using the General Household

Survey, the median duration of cohabitation appears to be somewhere in the vicinity of two years.[5] Only sixteen per cent of the cohabiting women had been living with that person for over five years. For those who would like to think that temporary cohabitation is not really much different from marriages that end in divorce, it is worth noting that the median length of marriages *that end in divorce* is ten years[6]—and most marriages do not end in divorce, even these days.

The Kiernan and Estaugh study also revealed that cohabiting mothers are poorly educated, (43 per cent have no educational qualifications, compared to 25 per cent of married mothers),[7] are two and a half times as likely as married mothers to be living in council housing,[8] almost five times more likely than married mothers to have an unemployed partner, and are somewhat *less* likely than married mothers to be working themselves.[9] Given all this, it may come as a surprise to learn that the average gross weekly income of cohabiting mothers is 86 per cent that of married mothers—£283 compared to £328.[10] The main difference is that cohabiting mothers are almost four times as likely as married mothers to report gross weekly incomes of £100 or less.

In McRae's study, cohabiting women who responded to questionnaire items about how they spend their leisure time, share obligations with their partner, and whether they are happy in life, gave answers that were much the same as the answers of married women. There was only one big difference in McRae's results: among cohabiting mothers who had not married, only 56 per cent would choose the same partner again if they could live their lives over, compared with 78 per cent of married women who had not cohabited before marriage,[11] suggesting a widespread dissatisfaction with the relationships. Unfortunately, none of the data in either study tackled the most problematic issue: what does cohabitation mean for a child? Does the man behave as married fathers behave? How is the psychological development of the child affected, compared to the child of married parents? Here, the research still consists of unfilled blanks.

Combining everything—illegitimacy, divorce, and cohabitation—the upshot is a portrait of the family that worked out this way in the 1991 census: 75 per cent of all English families with dependent children were headed by a married couple, 19 per cent were headed

by a lone parent, and 6 per cent were headed by a cohabiting couple. This is a cross-section, based on children who might be anywhere from infants to their late teens, and including children of divorce. For families with children born in 1991, 70 per cent were born to married couples, 16 per cent were born to unmarried couples living at the same address, and 14 per cent were born to a woman living alone.[12]

That is the picture for all of society, which already represents a huge change from earlier decades. But this overall picture looks much different when we introduce the role of social class.

Family Structure and Social Class

There is a natural tendency to assume that changes in family structure are linked with modernity. It makes sense that the pace of modern life, secularisation, and atomised nature of the city would combine to produce more divorces, more illegitimacy, more cohabitation, and fewer marriages.

But the empirical connection is not as clear as intuition says it should be. Take another look at the graph showing illegitimacy from the 1500s up to the present, and focus on the period from 1850-1900. It would be hard to find a time or place in which industrialisation and urbanisation were faster, more sweeping, or more wrenching than in Victorian England. And yet during that same period, illegitimacy went down, not up (crime also dropped, amazingly). The Victorian middle class was superbly efficient at propagating its values throughout society, and its success overcame the naturally disruptive forces of modernisation.

Trying to say that family breakdown is an 'inevitable part of modern life' also runs into problems when it is applied to contemporary England. The 1991 census provided data on the living arrangements of households with dependent children for each of the 403 local authorities in England and Wales. When one tries to match these numbers against the type of local authority, at first the results seem to match expectations. The local authorities in inner London fit the stereotype, showing the country's lowest percentage of married couples in households with dependent children (57 per cent). But in outer London, which is certainly counted as 'urbanised', 75 per cent of such households consist of married couples. The local authorities classified as 'remoter, largely rural' have one of the highest proportions of married couples (81 per cent), consistent with expectations. But marriage is even more prevalent (82 per cent) in the local authorities classified as 'mixed urban-rural'.[13] What lies behind these inconsistent results? Social class.

Since the early part of the century, English sociologists and demographers have used a five-class system to categorize occupations, and referred to them as 'social classes'. Class I consists of persons in the professions, Class II of those in technical and managerial positions, Class III of skilled occupations, Class IV of partly skilled occupations, and Class V of unskilled occupations. Each census reports the number of households in each of the 403 local authorities that fall into each class.

Suppose we take a very simple measure of a local authority's overall 'social class', the percentage of households in Class V, and compare it to the percentage of illegitimate births. Figure 3 (p. 129) shows what the relationship looks like for births in 1991.

You are looking at what is, for the social sciences, an extraordinarily regular relationship, with a correlation of +.70 on a scale of -1 to +1. I have labelled some of the local authorities at the extremes to give you a sense of what the dots mean. The basic statement is that births out of wedlock bear a strong relationship to social class. The lower the social class, the higher the proportion of births out of wedlock. The difference is extremely large. In the ten local authorities with the lowest percentage of households in Class V, 18 per cent of the children were born out of wedlock in 1991. In the ten local authorities with the highest percentage of households in Class V, 40 per cent of the children were born out of wedlock.

The extremes illustrate a more general point. The story that emerges from a more complete statistical analysis is that the England that still retains the two-parent family as the norm is not just the remnants of a by-gone rural, thatched-roof England, but communities that are characterised by high education and affluence. The England in which the family has effectively collapsed does not consist just of blacks, or even the inner-city neighbourhoods of London, Manchester, and Liverpool, but lower-working-class communities everywhere.

You may be wondering whether the same thing happens when we look at social class from the other end of the glass: Do local authorities with the most people in Classes I and II (professionals and managers) have the fewest illegitimate babies? The answer is yes, but the relationship is not as strong. Sidestepping the statistical details, it is somewhat more important that a local authority has few people at the very bottom than that it has many people at the top.

You may also ask whether the picture looks different if I stop focusing on illegitimacy and instead include single parents of all kinds. Perhaps the rich get married more often than the poor, but they split up more often too. But it doesn't work that way. On the contrary, divorce rates are higher among the working-class than among the middle and upper classes.

The New Victorians and the New Rabble

In short, breakdown in the English family is occurring in drastically different ways in different parts of English society. That relationship of social class to family is pregnant with a variety of possibilities for the future, none of them good.

To illustrate what has been happening since the 1970s, I first selected the districts with at least 95 per cent white population in the 1991 census, so that we could focus on the main issues (race is a minor factor in English illegitimacy).[14] I chose the ten districts which had the highest proportion of Class V households in both the 1981 and 1991 censuses. Examples of these districts were Middlesbrough, its neighbour Hartlepool, and Liverpool. Then I chose the ten districts that had the lowest proportion of Class V households. Examples included Wokingham, Surrey Heath, and South Buckinghamshire, bywords for the home of the professionals and executives that constitute what I am calling the 'upper middle class'.

Figure 4 (p. 130) shows the average proportion of children born out of wedlock in each group of districts from 1974 through 1991.

In 1974, just before the illegitimacy ratio had begun its steep climb, the overriding reality about English families was that the two-parent family prevailed everywhere. Even in the twenty districts with the highest percentages of unskilled workers, only 11 per cent of children were born out of wedlock in 1974, and they represented the high end of the range. The lower-class neighbourhoods in Middlesbrough, with many low-skilled workers and the upper-class neighbourhoods of Wokingham, with very few, were worlds apart economically and socially then as now. Besides being much poorer, residents in those neighbourhoods of Middlesbrough also typically ate different food, read different books, studied different courses in school, spoke in different accents, and in a hundred other ways lived lives that were different from lives in the affluent areas of Woking-ham. But in both communities, the two-parent family remained standard. The struggling Teessider and the economically secure Wokinghamian used the same social template.

By extension, all sorts of other things were similar about the two types of district as well. Stop and think for a moment about how intimately the institutions of a neighbourhood, including everything from how to get enough people to show up at a local charity drive to the rhythms of business at a pub, are shaped by the structure of the families there. The point for now is not whether they are well or badly shaped; just that they *are* shaped. Life is profoundly different in communities where the building block is the household consisting of a husband and wife and housing areas where large proportions of households consist of adults living singly or together temporarily.

Switch to 1991. Now, there are areas in Middlesbrough (with 45 per cent of its births out of wedlock), and areas of Wokingham (with 15 per cent) that no longer use the same social template, and this may be generalised to the top and bottom of English society. This does not mean that all is well in Wokingham; but Wokingham is a place where society is still organised on the basis of the two-parent family, and Middlesbrough is a place that contains areas where the norms of two-parent family life have already been replaced by something else. In that abstract phrase, 'the norms of family life', lies a complicated bundle of values that can bind a society together when they are shared across social classes, and split it apart when they are not.

Figure 4 uses the only available data, based on district-level totals. Suppose instead that we could draw these lines for individuals in the low-skilled working class and the upper middle class? And suppose that we could extend them to the year 2000? There are two scenarios, one widely held by the journalists, academics, and social welfare officials with whom I talked (and they included some highly astute observers), and another that nonetheless seems to me more probable.

Scenario I begins from the premise that the breakdown of the traditional family is a part of modernisation that cannot be reversed, and that the data for communities and individuals look about the same. Many among the intelligentsia think this is a good thing. The English family is not deteriorating, they cheerfully report, but merely changing. I spoke with others who were less sanguine, but they too were convinced that nothing much can be done about it. If this logic is correct, then illegitimacy will continue to increase in the upper middle class. In fact, the rate of increase should begin to match or surpass that of the lower classes as the old conventions which have held back the upper middle class fade. The future would look something like Scenario I, A Brave New World, (p. 131).

While a gap may continue to separate the upper middle class from the low-skilled working class, it will not be very many years before the norms of family life will once again be shared by people across the social spectrum. In that case, it is safe to predict that English society will be dysfunctional in ways that can now be only dimly imagined, but at least all the social classes will be suffering from the same problems.

An alternative scenario is possible, which looks like Scenario II, The New Victorians and the New Rabble, (p. 131).

The first distinctive feature of Scenario II is that it shows a gap between low-skilled working class and upper-middle-class *individuals* that is already much greater than the gap between lower-class and upper-middle-class *communities*. This is an extrapolation from America, where close analysis has always shown that the relationship between socioeconomic class and illegitimacy becomes much stronger as the focus shifts from communities to the individual. When the illegitimacy ratio goes up in a generally affluent American suburb, it is predominantly caused by daughters of the Class IV and Class V households who live in that otherwise affluent suburb. Specifically: white American women who grow up in Class V households have five times the illegitimacy ratio of women from Class I households.[15]

Based on indirect evidence, a similar relationship seems to hold true in England. Individual-level data reveal that English unmarried mothers are much more poorly educated and have lower incomes than married mothers or unmarried women without children, for example.[16] But I am really interested in the social class of the parents of unmarried mothers. A study conducted in Tayside comes a bit closer to this, showing that the teenage pregnancy rate for girls from the poorest neighbourhoods was six times the rate for teenagers from the more affluent neighbourhoods. The actual ratio of births was even higher, because girls from the poorest areas were less likely to have an abortion.[17]

The gap between English social classes is thus likely to be already larger than the data from the districts show. How much larger?

Conservatively applying the American relationships (as I have done in preparing the Scenario II figure), in 1991 English daughters of Class I families were having only about 11 per cent of their children out of wedlock, compared to 45 per cent among daughters of Class V families.

We will probably find out how close this estimate is within a matter of months. Existing English databases on individuals can address the issue directly, and I am told that studies are in progress. The actual figures will no doubt differ from a direct extrapolation of the American experience, but they are unlikely to overturn the general expectation: the gap between the lower and upper-middle class communities shown in Scenario II is substantially greater at the individual level than at the community level and has been increasing rapidly.

The other distinctive feature of the second scenario is that I show illegitimacy levelling off, and even declining, among the upper middle class. This is why I talk about the 'New Victorians' and the 'New Rabble', meaning that one part of society—the affluent, well-educated part—will edge back towards traditional morality while a large portion of what used to be the British working class goes the way of the American underclass. Given the day-to-day evidence that the upper classes are in a state of moral disarray, this may seem an odd prediction, but there are reasons for it.

The New Victorians

I begin from the premise that the traditional monogamous marriage with children is in reality, on average, in the long run, the most satisfying way to live a human life. Or, as a cynic might put it, marriage with children is the worst way to live a human life except for all the others.

Marriage does not need to be propped up either by governments or propagandists. Left alone, marriage emerges everywhere, in all societies, and evolves toward monogamy. Marriage can, however, be undermined. For the last quarter century, marriage has been under assault from two broad directions. One is cultural, and has been linked (unnecessarily, it will prove in the long run) with feminism. The other is economic—it has become more expensive to raise children within marriage, less expensive to raise children outside it.

For the upper middle class, the effects of the economic assault are difficult to assess. The extremely high marginal tax rates of the

1970s may well have been relevant to calculations of marriage and childbearing, but the incomes of the upper middle class have been above the level where changes in the benefit system itself can reasonably be expected to have changed the attractiveness of marriage. But the cultural assault took its toll. In the 1970s and the 1980s, marriage and its core values—especially involving fidelity and parenthood—were unfashionable and often frankly scorned. One who got married in that era could chalk up few psychic points in his or her internal book-keeping for extramarital temptations resisted and parental duties fulfilled. On the contrary, to resist temptation was more commonly thought to be a sign of a repressed personality and doggedly to fulfil duties toward spouse and children was a sign of someone who was awfully boring.

But the cultural assault was bound to be temporary. It could not sustain itself because much of the assault consisted of sociological marriage-bashing that did not correspond with reality. The proposition that marriage is *typically* coercive, exploitative, and joyless is not true. Yes, there is such a thing as spouse abuse, but, defined in any serious way, it is statistically uncommon. Yes, strict divorce laws used to trap some people in unhappy marriages, but English married life prior to 1971 was not a sea of misery. Yes, marriages have their boring stretches and fidelity sometimes wavers; but people who have known a good marriage wouldn't trade it for anything and many who haven't known a good marriage are conscious of what they are missing. As time goes on, the cultural assault on marriage has receded and will continue to recede, for the most basic of reasons: at bottom, the marriage-bashers got it wrong.

Besides that, sexual restraint is about to make a comeback, at least in some social circles. It may not seem that way as you read this week's lingerie ads in the Sunday papers, but this particular prophecy is not really a tough call. Sexual modes are notorious for swinging like a pendulum, as English history has so often demonstrated so colourfully, and among the safest of bets is that licentiousness will be followed by puritanism.

But I need not rely solely on historical precedent. The natural rebound is getting a powerful generational shove in the 1990s. The birth cohort that came of age in the late 1960s and early 1970s, with its remarkable power to define the *zeitgeist* that it has enjoyed for three decades, began turning 40 in the late 1980s. Lo and behold, the attitudes of its members have been changing accordingly. They are less mesmerised by their careers, more concerned about children and community. Free sexual expression is no longer quite such a big deal. As they reach fifty, which will begin to happen in just a few years, another change will occur, as they suddenly become aware that the end of life is no longer just a theoretical possibility. Questions about the meaning of life and religion that they were quick to dismiss in their thirties will be called up for re-examination. They will rediscover, no doubt with that irritating solipsism that has been the hallmark of their generation, that the deepest, most nourishing ways of thinking about the problems of mortality and spiritual concerns are to be found in some very old texts called the Bible and the *Nichomachean Ethics*.

Some likely consequences of this rediscovery within the upper middle class will be a revival of religion and of the intellectual respectability of concepts such as fidelity, courage, loyalty, self-restraint, moderation, and other admirable human qualities that until lately have barely dared speak their names. These changes will have sweeping effects on the national received wisdom, and on various behaviours. It seems likely that divorce among the upper middle class will fall, for example. The children of the upper middle class will be raised by parents who teach traditional lessons about marriage and parenthood, and those lessons will 'take' among increasing numbers of those children, once again for the most basic of reasons: they are true. And from all this comes my earlier prediction that the illegitimacy ratio among the upper middle class will begin to rise more slowly, then begin to go down.

Is there any evidence that such a phenomenon might already be under way? Using district-level data, no. The rate of increase in illegitimacy among the upper-middle-class districts as shown in the opening figure has been about the same for the last half-dozen years. Individual data on the social class of the father for jointly-registered illegitimate births also show a steady increase in the proportion of Class I and Class II births that are jointly registered out-of-wedlock instead of legitimate.[18] The notion that illegitimacy among the upper middle class will eventually decrease is a pure prediction, not an extrapolation from existing trends.

This forecast is not limited exclusively to what I have called the upper middle class of professionals and executives. Presumably the middle class will also share in the New Victorianism, as will the skilled working-class. But further down the social ladder, among the low-skill (and low-income) working class, Scenario II assumes that there will be increasing recruitment into the underclass. This brings us to the New Rabble.

The New Rabble

Illegitimacy in the lower classes will continue to rise and, inevitably, life in lower class communities will continue to degenerate—more crime, more widespread drug and alcohol addiction, fewer marriages, more dropout from work, more homelessness, more child neglect, fewer young people pulling themselves out of the slums, more young people tumbling in.

Why do I assume that these bad outcomes have anything to do with the growth in illegitimacy? This was a subject of vigorous debate even before John Redwood threw down the gauntlet in July 1993. The early salvos had been fired by social critics on the right, led by Digby Anderson, and had therefore been widely discounted by social policy intelligentsia as left-over Thatcherism. But then one of the most respected English sociologists and a man of the left, Professor A.H. Halsey, publicly called attention to the dangers of rising illegitimacy. His warnings were followed by a broadside from sociologists Norman Dennis and George Erdos, both ethical socialists. Their 1992 Institute of Economic Affairs treatise *Families Without Fatherhood* provoked in turn outraged responses asserting that it was poverty, not single parenthood, that was really responsible for any problems that children of lone mothers might have.[19] Norman Dennis has since published a follow-up, *Rising Crime and the Dismembered Family*, that expanded his review of the earlier research and was surgically effective in exposing the misuse of the existing research by his opponents.[20]

I was surprised last autumn to find that this battle still has to be fought. Given the studies already available, it seems odd that academics with professional reputations to worry about are still disputing the basic point that, *ceteris paribus*, the two-parent family is a superior environment for the nurturing of children. I understand that ideology plays an important part in this debate, but there is also such a thing as the weight of the data, and this is not a subject on which the direction of the findings is in technical dispute.

Watching the debate from an American vantage point, another obvious fact is that the English returns, damning as they already are, are just beginning to come in. England is in the predicament of Wile

E. Coyote, having run off the edge of a cliff at high speed and, for a time, unaware that he is suspended above the abyss. All of the English studies of the effects of single-parenthood are based on children who grew up in the 1960s and 1970s, when the overall number of single-parent children in low-income communities was low. That is, the extant English studies are showing the costs of single-parenthood *in communities where single parenthood is rare.* Those disadvantages are real, but they are nothing compared to the costs that multiply in communities where single parenthood has become common. American scholars have had time to observe those additional consequences, which is why there is no longer an American scholarly debate about whether single parenthood has large social costs.

But these remarks about the technical literature are probably beside the point here, because there is no way to demonstrate the state of knowledge with a few snappy statistics. Those who cling to 'the family is not deteriorating but changing' line would not be persuaded, and those who think the socially destructive effects of illegitimacy are already palpable need no further persuasion. For now, I am addressing the latter group, and asking you to imagine an England in which the New Victorianism has taken hold in the upper middle class, while at the same time the New Rabble is making life in low-skill working-class communities ever more chaotic and violent.

A few concrete results seem likely. Physical segregation of the classes will become more extreme. Two-parent working-class families will increasingly leave council housing, and council housing will increasingly be the place where the underclass congregates (a process which is already well-advanced in many cities). This will in turn have effects on local businesses. One of the ways in which England still remains distinctive from the United States is that the most notorious London council estates co-exist within a few blocks of thriving shopping areas. This will gradually end and the American model for the inner-city—rows of boarded-up shops, an exodus of the chain stores, street-corner drug markets—will become more prevalent. As shops and offices are vacated, squatting will become more widespread, and so will fires. See photos of the South Bronx, commonly compared to post-blitz London, for a glimpse of the future.

The people who are able to afford it will move farther from the inner-city to be safe. The rich will tend to seek areas that are not only physically distant from the inner-city, but defensible. In the United

States the 'gated community', with its private security force and guardhouse at the restricted entrance, is the cheerless model that will increasingly be adopted in England.

New divisions will open up within the lower half of the socioeconomic distribution. I leave it to those who know the English class system better than I to spell out the possibilities in detail but, at some point along the continuum, a working class, probably skilled, consisting predominantly of two-parent families, will separate itself from a less-skilled, predominantly unmarried working class—politically, socially, geographically. Family structure will be a conscious point of division.

The current debate about crime and punishment will shift. Intellectual rhetoric that decries prisons may continue, but measures that keep convicted criminals in their own geographic communities through house detention, using electronic bracelets and other technological devices, will gain broader acceptance in upper middle class intellectual circles. Outside intellectual circles, the mood will become much more openly punitive and hostile toward criminals.

This bring us to the problem of money. The costs of the benefit system for single parents has already become a hot political issue, but the current controversy is nothing compared to the intense hostility that will develop within the near future. Whatever else you may think about illegitimacy, this much is indisputable: it costs money. As illegitimacy continues to rise, the costs will rise not just linearly, but by multiples, for so many things go together—not just the costs of single-parent benefit for young women and their children, but the costs of coping with young males who are not in the work force and are in the criminal justice system, of children abandoned and neglected, of increased drug addiction.

If the underclass that is to be isolated in this way were to consist of only a small proportion of the population, then the prospect for the country as a whole would not be grim. The New Victorianism I have described is an optimistic forecast for those who share in it, and if the underclass were to remain small, the increased costs, social and budgetary, would not be unbearable. But the English underclass is not going to be small.

In the United States, the downward plunge of the black inner city began in the last half of the 1960s, when the overall illegitimacy ratio among blacks moved past the 25 per cent range and the ratio in lower class communities was upwards of 40 per cent. If those proportions represent something like a 'critical mass' for transforming the social functioning of communities, then the prognosis is grim. England's overall illegitimacy ratio passed the 25 per cent point in 1988. In 1991, 8.5 per cent of the English population lived in districts where the illegitimacy ratio had passed 40 per cent. Within a few years, assuming a straight-line extension of the national trend, a quarter of the English population will live in districts with more than 40 per cent of births out of wedlock. The implication is that we are not talking about a small underclass, but a very large one.

At this point, what has already been speculative becomes too uncertain even to guess at. How will the Labour Party evolve as its old supporters are increasingly divided between a single-parent constituency that constantly presses for more benefits and a two-parent working class that is increasingly willing to distance itself from that constituency? How will the Conservative Party evolve if the social environment shifts toward the New Victorianism I have described? What new political force, neither left nor right but authoritarian and repressive, might emerge?

Whatever the specifics, this conclusion seems appropriate. English society has for centuries been a supreme example of civil society, in two senses: 'civil' in terms of the uncoerced social norms of daily life, and 'civil' in that England was the original home of Western liberty, the country where neither the military nor police in any form were the chief instruments of social order. Under the scenario I have described, English civility in both senses is doomed.

Perverse Policy

Such a gloomy conclusion. And why is it necessary? After all, I am envisioning a renaissance of Victorian values elsewhere in English society. Why shouldn't lower class communities also share in the New Victorianism and see the family start to revive? The answer? Because British social policy, unless radically changed, will systematically sustain the disintegration of the family in low income groups.

A System Designed to Be Exploited

I met the man I will call Scully on an overspill estate on the outskirts of Liverpool—the capital of Britain's black economy— where he helped me navigate some of the rougher council estates. By the end of the day, Scully had decided I was painfully naïve. We ducked into a pub to wait out a rainstorm, and he went about setting me straight.

Scully has two school-age children, both by the same woman. She has £80 a week for herself, £80 a month for the children, plus her housing benefit, and Scully has £88 a fortnight in income support. Then there is the arrangement with his mate who putatively rents a room in the flat that Scully rents, though of course Scully doesn't actually live there. That dodge nets Scully another £100 a month after splitting with his mate. It adds up to £276 in cash for him every month, £400 for his woman, plus free housing. Figure the housing is worth about £200. Then there's the break on the council tax, free school meals and uniforms for the kids, and a variety of other bits and pieces. Total value? Somewhere between £900 and £1,000 per month—referring, of course, to income on which Scully and the woman pay no tax. That isn't his entire income, of course. He has an off-the-books job in Birmingham, where he spends most of each week, returning to the north at weekends to see the family and to register for the dole. Scully's total income puts him far beyond temptation by any job he could hope to get.

Scully doesn't worry about getting caught. There are many ways of getting around the system, some of them quite sophisticated. But don't the Social Security people know about the same tricks? Sure, Scully says. But they don't care, as long as you don't rub their nose in it. You have to know when abuse of the system becomes so blatant that the bureaucracy must take notice of it. That's the key, I am told later by a person who has worked in a benefit office. The attitude of the people who run the local benefit offices is that 'as long as it's going to the right people'—the downtrodden working class—these dodges and scams are not so important. Besides which, it's not worth their time to prosecute. What can they recover even if the prosecution is successful? The worst that is likely to happen to Scully is having his income support cancelled.

Does Scully feel any guilt about anything he's doing? 'The system's there to be f***ed', he said. 'You're soft if you don't'. How unusual is Scully? 'I know more people like me than people who are actually working', he answered. I asked him to tell me about his friends who were playing the system straight. After a long pause, he said, 'I'm not making this up. I can't think of anyone'. Another pause. 'One person. My mother.'

No one seems to know whether we can take Scully's account at face value. The Inland Revenue attributes about six to eight per cent of GDP to the black economy, which could amount to about £50 billion.[21] In 1992, Department of Employment inspectors forced 50,000 people to withdraw benefit claims, but such figures do not tell us how common unemployment fraud is. The closest I have found to such a figure involves minicab drivers at Heathrow Airport: of 150 interviewed by inspectors in July 1992, 107—72 per cent—had to withdraw unemployment claims.[22] More systematic studies of fraud are said to be under way. Even this one example suggests that Scully is not too far off the mark.

In any case, I am not trying to draw up an indictment of the Employment Service. My point refers to the reality that faces a young man in today's low-skill working-class neighbourhoods. Does he live in a world where large numbers of his mates are fiddling the system successfully, and where your neighbours and peers no longer consider it a moral black mark against you? If that is the case—and it is hard to believe that anyone is really prepared to argue otherwise—then, judged from the time horizon and the priorities of young adulthood, it is foolish to marry.

The Economics of Illegitimacy

Is the answer to rid the benefit system of fraud and abuse? Not really. The scandal of the current system is not what you get if you cheat, but what you get if you play it straight. I began with Scully's story because it is probably the one that is most realistic. But suppose instead that we imagine a pristine benefit system and utterly honest clients. The story is just about as heavily loaded against marriage as it is for a rogue like Scully. Here are the economic facts of life facing a fictitious pair of honest young people—let's call them Ross and Stacey—who are in their late teens and have been keeping company. The numbers are courtesy of sociologist Patricia Morgan, who is preparing a study of the benefit system to be published by the IEA.[23]

Stacey has discovered she is pregnant. She didn't do it on purpose—I am not appealing to the image of the young woman who gets pregnant to get a council flat. Blame it on the sexual revolution, if you wish, or nature having its way as it has with young people forever. Stacey would just as soon not have an abortion, if she can afford to take care of the baby. She and Ross sit down and have a talk.

Ross has a job paying £228 a week (close to the median for manual workers in 1991, and better than most unskilled young men just getting started).[24] After taking into account deductions for income tax, national insurance, rent and community charges, then adding in their family credit and all other pertinent means-tested or universal benefits, Ross and Stacey and the baby will have an after-tax net of about £152.

But suppose they don't get married. Then, they will have £216— £74 in benefit for Stacey and the baby, none of it taxed, plus Ross's after-tax income as a single unmarried person, which amounts to about £142. Their weekly premium for not marrying is £64 a week, £3,328 a year, a 'raise' of 42 per cent over their married income. As Scully might say, Ross and Stacey would have to be soft to get married.

If Ross is unemployed, Stacey has even less incentive to marry, for the most obvious of reasons. Before, at least Ross had a job and prospects for the future. Without a job, Ross has no attractions as a future provider. Even in the present, he is worth less as a husband than as a live-in lover. Adding up the income support for a couple with one infant and the family premium, they would have £94 a week, plus a council flat. But if they *don't* get married, the same benefit package will amount to £108—a difference of £14 a week. Little as it may seem to those for whom such sums are pocket money, it amounts to a raise of 15 per cent over the income they would have if they married.

There are other advantages to claiming income support separately. The benefits of one cannot be reduced to pay off the other's debts as long as they are unmarried. This sounds especially good to Stacey, seeing that Ross is a bit irresponsible in money matters. If Stacey wants to supplement her income after the baby is born, the first £15 of her earnings will be disregarded when computing her benefit—three times the 'disregard' if she is married. All in all, Stacey has no economic reason whatsoever to swallow her doubts about Ross and try to get him to marry her. Staying single makes sense for her. As for Ross, why not remain free? He knows very well he has a wandering eye. He's in the full flood of young male adulthood. *Why get married?*

This is the first reason why the New Victorianism will not percolate down to the New Rabble. In the low-skilled working class, marriage makes no sense. *Of course* a high proportion of young women from low-income neighbourhoods and their boyfriends don't get married now. Even higher proportions won't get married in the future, as the illegitimacy ratio in low-income neighbourhoods continues to be pushed by this persistent economic reality.

The Next Generation

This is not the whole story, however. The *local* cultural norms in low-skilled working-class communities are likely to continue to deteriorate, even after the New Victorianism is in full bloom elsewhere—because the next generation will know no other way to think.

When I wrote about the nascent British underclass five years ago, I briefly referred to young males as 'essentially barbarians' who are civilised by marriage. Since then, that image has become all too literal in the American inner city, where male teenage behaviour is often a caricature of the barbarian male: retaliate against anyone who shows you the slightest disrespect ('disses' you). Sleep with and impregnate as many girls as possible. Violence is a sign of strength. To worry about tomorrow is weakness. To die young is glorious. What makes this trend so disturbing is not just that these principles describe behaviour, but that inner-city boys articulate them *as principles*. They are, explicitly, the code by which they live.

This comes as no surprise to observers who for many years have predicted what would become of a generation of fatherless boys. Adolescence and testosterone are a destructive combination, and the only antidote is a civilising process that begins in infancy and is completed by marriage. I am arguing that the civilising process *cannot* occur in communities where the two-parent family is not the norm, and this will turn out to be as true of England as America. The real problem with the 'alternative' of unmarried parenthood is that it offers no ethical alternative for socialising little boys. For males, the ethical code of the two-parent family is the only game in town.

To see what I mean, try to imagine a code of ethics that the unmarried mother can teach to her male children that excludes marriage. She can try to teach him to be honest, not to assault other people, to be self-reliant. But what shall she teach him about his responsibility toward his own children? What can she teach him about his responsibility to the mother of his children? There is no coherent code that both accepts the premise that having children entails a moral commitment by both the father and the mother, and yet manages to sidestep all the ways that a moral commitment must translate into something that looks very like the obligations of marriage.

If unmarried mothers all over England are assiduously teaching their little boys not to do as their fathers did, then perhaps the New Victorianism has a chance of percolating down to lower-class communities. Even then there would be problems, because children take a reality check on the lessons they are taught, and reality would be egregiously disparate from the lessons. But it is doubtful that even lip service is being paid to marriage. In 1989, the British Social Attitudes Survey asked respondents whether they agreed with the proposition that 'People who want children ought to get married'. Among those 65 and older, 92 per cent agreed. Among those ages 18-24, only 43 per cent agreed.[25]

If not even an 'ought' links children and marriage, then the foundation for socialising young males is gone. Perhaps, for form's sake, I should not focus so explicitly on males. No doubt there are interesting things to be said about the socialisation of young females when marriage ceases to be a central goal of life. But of all the many controversial issues that have been touched upon in this discussion, these are the questions that most need contemplation: How are males to be socialised if not by an ethic centred on marriage and family? And if they are not socialised, how may we expect the next generation of young English males to behave? In upper-middle-class communities where marriage never stopped being a norm, and if a traditional ethic revives as I have forecast, the prospects are bright. In lower class communities, where the norm of marriage has already effectively been lost and a generation of boys is growing up socialised by a 'something else' ethic not centred on marriage and family, it seems inconceivable to me that England can expect revival in the upper classes to have much effect. It is not just the economic head wind that will have to be bucked, but a cultural milieu that bears no resemblance to anything that English society has ever known.

What To Do

The debate over single mothers which began forthrightly in July of 1993 and escalated at the subsequent Conservative Conference has since descended into farce as Tory rhetoric about 'family values' ran headlong into spectacularly inapt Tory behaviour, epitomised but by no means limited to the Yeo and Milligan affairs. Even apart from those episodes, it became apparent after the leak of the Social Security White Paper in November that the Conservatives are of several minds about the lone mother problem, and that the ambivalence begins with John Major. Not much is going to happen under the present government except a few tepid reforms, tweaking a benefit level here and re-writing a regulation there, as often as not making single parenthood more attractive, not less (witness the latest proposal to offset childcare). Nor is there any reason to believe that a Labour victory would be followed by anything better. On the contrary, unmarried parents are well on their way to becoming Labour's most numerous constituency.

Nonetheless, the present era of political waffling is the right time for people who are not running for election to start debating more radical reforms, because this much is certain: within not many years, a political consensus for radical reform is going to coalesce. One way or another, England, like other Western democracies with soaring illegitimacy ratios, is approaching a time when the economy can no longer sustain generous benefit systems for unmarried mothers without a political revolt. This is the approaching budgetary reality even if you do not accept my forecast of rising hostility between the New Victorians and the New Rabble. Add in that hostility, and the pressures to reduce the costs of the benefit system are going to be explosive.

This means going back to first principles. The current phase of the policy debate need not worry about shaping a bill to be presented in the House of Commons this year, but can focus instead on a vigorous debate about how a civil, free society sustains itself, and the role that the family plays in that process. The purpose of this discussion has been to encourage such a debate.

What shape might the ultimately radical reforms take? A visitor from abroad is least able to make those judgements. Here are a few cautionary notes and general thoughts.

Full Employment

It seemed axiomatic to just about everyone I interviewed that full employment must be part of any solution to the illegitimacy problem. And it makes sense, up to a point. In 1991, the correlation between the male unemployment rate and the illegitimacy ratio in local authorities was a phenomenal +.85 (on a -1 to +1 scale). Furthermore, a highly plausible story links the rise of unemployment and illegitimacy in the late 1970s. Nonmarital sexual activity was high in the late 1970s. Girls got pregnant, but their boy friends, newly unemployed, became suddenly less attractive marriage partners. The same thing had happened in 1929, of course, but there was a big difference: in 1979, the benefit system for single mothers offered an alternative to marriage.

The problem is that, even though the combination of high unemployment and a generous benefit system of single mothers might have triggered the rise in illegitimacy, it does not follow that full employment will produce a fall in illegitimacy.

This is not just a logical objection. England conducted a natural experiment in the 1980s. Between the 1981 and 1991 censuses, male unemployment went up in 196 English and Welsh districts, and down in 205 districts. The swings were large, ranging up to 18 percentage points on the male unemployment rate. If full employment were going to restore the two-parent family, there should have been at least some change for the better in the districts where young men were getting jobs. What happened? Illegitimacy increased *more* in districts where the employment of males improved than in districts where it got worse.[26] This is true no matter how the data are sliced, but it is most intriguingly, if depressingly, true of districts where the unemployment was worst in 1981. Throughout England and Wales, 60 districts in 1981 were suffering from more than 15 per cent unemployment among men. In 1991, 47 of those 60 districts had a lower unemployment rate. Their illegitimacy ratios had gone up by an average of 23 percentage points in the intervening ten years, far above the national average of 17 points. This was true even of the districts (such as Corby and Derwentside) where the improvement in employment was dramatically large.

Full employment is a fine goal, and achieving it will surely facilitate marriage. But, based on the experience of the 1980s, there is no reason to suppose that improving the employment picture is by itself going to have any effect on changes in illegitimacy.[27]

The Minimalist Solution: Stop Penalising Marriage

At the very least, stop making the benefit system favour single mothers over married mothers. It is easy enough to do. Establish income support and family benefit levels such that any married couple receives a benefit at least as large as any benefit that can be obtained outside marriage, given the same number of children and employment situation, under any visible or concealed living arrangements with boyfriend or girlfriend.

Note the proviso, 'visible or concealed'. The financial benefit for married couples must match the *best* financial situation in which an unmarried mother could find herself, which means that married couples with an unemployed husband will end up in a better financial situation than a single mother with no boyfriend. Otherwise, the system retains a clear and present incentive for single women with boyfriends to remain unmarried and represent themselves to the benefit office as women living alone.

This solution is minimalist in both its implementation and effects. It would require only changes in benefit levels, not in the basic machinery of the benefit system. But it is also doubtful whether, by itself, the changes would be decisive. Marriage would no longer be a financially punishing decision, but having a baby out of wedlock would become no more painful.

In terms of budgets, the minimalist solution will be hugely expensive if it is achieved by raising the benefits for married couples instead of lowering the benefits for single parents. I will leave the detailed calculations to the budget experts, but I doubt that England can afford to increase the benefits for married couples enough to eliminate the penalties of marriage if it retains its current benefit levels for single women. This leaves us with the question: What kind of system might be both affordable and restore marriage as the framework for having children?

Facing Up to Hard Choices

A number of strategies *could* work, given the political will. American social critic Mickey Kaus has recently proposed a solution that would replace the entire American welfare system with guaranteed public service jobs at slightly below the prevailing market wage. Many years ago, Milton Friedman proposed replacing the entire welfare system with a negative income tax—a guaranteed income—that would replace all other benefits. I favour eliminating benefits for unmarried women altogether (for potential new entrants, while keeping the Faustian bargain we have made with women already on the system). A strong case can be made that any of these radical changes would produce large reductions in the number of children born to single women. The simplest of all solutions for England that might have a major positive effect? Simply restore the benefit structure (in constant pounds) that you had in 1960.

The time has not yet come to try to make such arguments in detail. Before a debate over any of these alternatives can take place meaningfully (in the United States as in England, I should add), a few hard truths that people have preferred to ignore must be confronted:

The real rewards of marriage are long-term and intangible, but the seductive temptations not to marry for young people are short-term and concrete. In the past, the laws of economics imposed unbearable economic penalties on an unmarried woman with a small child. She was not an economically viable unit. Society backstopped the economic pain with immediate and concrete social penalties. The combination led women to make insistent demands on any man who wanted to sleep with them. Society backstopped those demands by holding out to men one glitteringly attractive and tangible reward: marriage was the only socially acceptable way to have regular sexual access to a woman. It was often the only way, period. Marriage flourished.

It is unlikely, even with the New Victorianism, that extramarital sex will ever subside to the point that the sexual motive for marriage will regain its once sovereign power. But the latent economic penalties of unmarried parenthood are as natural now as ever. The House of Commons does not need to legislate artificial ones. They will occur of their own accord, even in this liberated age, because it remains true now as before that a young single adult human trying to make a living and also to raise a small child is taking on more than one adult human being can easily do. It is a lot easier with two adult human beings sharing the burden. That's the way the world works, until the state intervenes. The state should stop intervening, and let the natural economic penalties occur.

The penalties may occur in the context of a welfare state. It is possible to have a social safety net that protects everyone from cradle to grave, as long as a social contract is accepted. The government will provide protection against the vicissitudes of life as long as you, the individual citizen, take responsibility for the consequences of your own voluntary behaviour. Getting pregnant and bearing a child is, at the present time, voluntary behaviour.

Many will find even this level of restraint on the welfare state unacceptable. But as you cast about for solutions, I suggest that one must inevitably come up against this rock. The welfare of society requires that women actively avoid getting pregnant if they have no husband, and that women once again demand marriage from a man who would have them bear a child. The only way the active avoidance and the demands are going to occur is if childbearing entails economic penalties for a single woman. It is all horribly sexist, I know. It also happens to be true.

Other things happen to be true as well. Babies need fathers. Society needs fathers. The stake for England, as for the United States, is not to be measured in savings in the Social Security budget nor in abstract improvements in the moral climate. The stake is the survival of free institutions and a civil society.

Figure 1
Percentage of Children Born to Unmarried Women 1540-1991

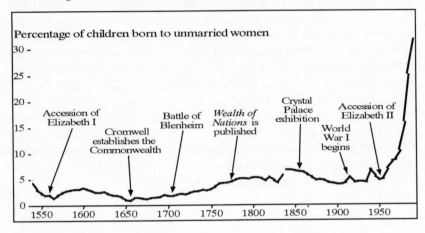

Laslett *et al.*, 1980, Table 1.1, OPCS, *Birth Statistics*, FM1 no. 13, Table 1.1., FM20, Table 1.1.

Figure 2
Divorces, 1961-1991

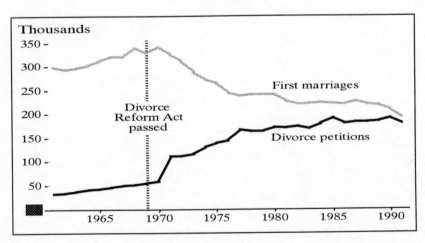

Source: OPCS, *Marriage and Divorce Statistics*, 1993, Table 2.1 and comparable earlier editions. (Marriage refers to first marriages for both bride and groom.)

129

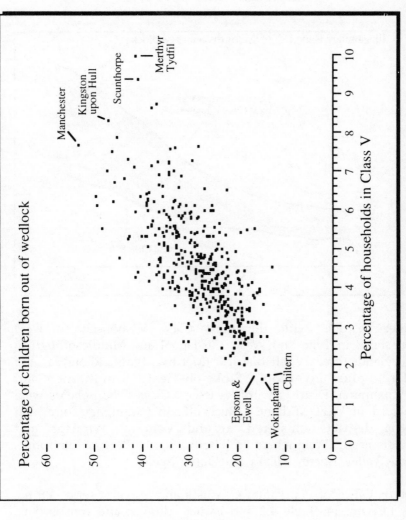

Children Born out of Wedlock and Social Class, 1991

Percentage of children born out of wedlock

Percentage of households in Class V

Manchester

Kingston
upon Hull

Scunthorpe

Merthyr
Tydfil

Epsom &
Ewell

Wokingham

Chiltern

Source: 1991 Census data, County Reports, Table 90, and Office of Population Censuses and Surveys, 1993b, Table 4.2

130

Figure 4
Illegitimacy Ratio 1974-1991

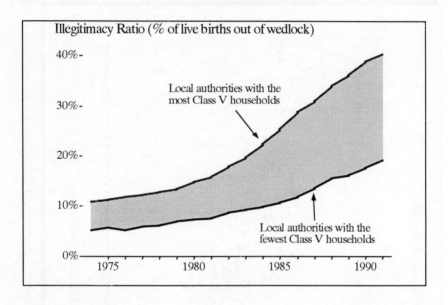

Note: Districts with the most Class V households were Gateshead in Tyne and Wear, Hartlepool and Middlesbrough in Cleveland, three Welsh districts (Merthyr Tydfil, Rhondda, and Afan), plus Liverpool, Stoke-on-Trent, Scunthorpe, and Southampton. Districts with the fewest Class V households were Solihull in West Midlands, Rushcliffe in Nottinghamshire, and eight districts clustered around London: Windsor and Maidenhead, Wokingham, Chiltern, South Bucks, Elmbridge, Mole Valley, Surrey Heath and Tandridge.

Source: Office of Population Censuses and Surveys, series VS no. 18, PP1 no. 14, Table 4.2 and earlier editions, and census data, County Reports for the 1981 and 1991 censuses.

Figure 5

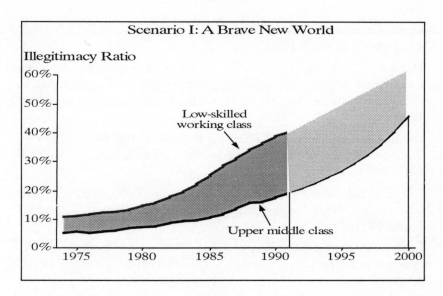

Scenario I: A Brave New World

Illegitimacy Ratio

Low-skilled working class

Upper middle class

Figure 6

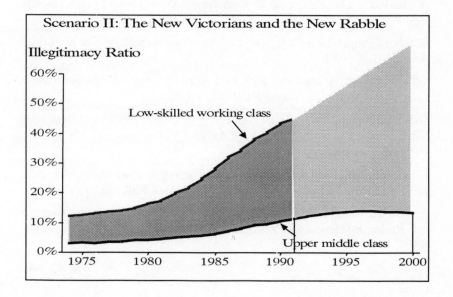

Scenario II: The New Victorians and the New Rabble

Illegitimacy Ratio

Low-skilled working class

Upper middle class

132

Bibliography

Central Statistical Office, *Annual Abstract of Statistics 1993*, No. 129 ed., London: HMSO, 1993.

Dennis, N., *Rising Crime and the Dismembered Family: How Conformist Intellectuals have Campaigned Against Common Sense*, Choice in Welfare, No. 18, London: IEA Health and Welfare Unit, 1993.

Dennis, N. and Erdos, G., *Families Without Fatherhood*, Choice in Welfare, No. 12, second edition, London: IEA Health and Welfare Unit, 1993.

Kiernan, K.E. and Estaugh, V., *Cohabitation: Extra-marital Child-bearing and Social Policy*, Family Policy Studies Centre, Occasional Paper 17, 1993.

Laslett, P., Oosterveen, K. and Smith, R.M., (ed), *Bastardy and Its Comparative History*, Cambridge, MA: Harvard University Press, 1980.

McRae, S., *Co-habiting Mothers: Changing Marriage and Motherhood?*, London: Policy Studies Institute, 1993.

Murray, C., *The Emerging British Underclass,* London: IEA Health and Welfare Unit, 1990.

Office of Population Censuses and Surveys, *Key Statistics for Local Authorities*, 1981.

Office of Population Censuses and Surveys, *1991 Birth Statistics: England and Wales,* Series FM2, no. 20, 1993.

Office of Population Censuses and Surveys, *1991 Key Population and Vital Statistics: Local and Health Authority Areas,* Series VS, no. 18, PP1, no. 14, 1993.

Office of Population Censuses and Surveys, *1991 Marriage and Divorce Statistics: England and Wales*, Series FM2, no. 19, 1993.

Smith, T., 'Influence of Socio-economic Factors on Attaining Targets for Reducing Teenage Pregnancies', *British Medical Journal*, no. 6887, 1993.

Notes

1   *Office of Population Censuses and Surveys,* 1981, Table 7.

2   *1991 Census Report for Great Britain (Part I),* Table 8, pp. 194-195.

3   Walker, A., 'Blaming the Victims', in Murray, C., *The Emerging British Underclass,* Choice in Welfare Series No. 2, London: IEA Health & Welfare Unit, 1990.

4   McRae, S., 1993, Figure 1, p. 20. Of the 38 women of the study who were living alone, six had been married and then divorced in the four-and-a-half year follow-up, representing 4 per cent of all cohabiting mothers in the study.

5   Kiernan and Estaugh, 1993, Table 2.5.

6   OPCS, *1991 Marriage and Divorce Statistics,* 1993, Table 4.3.

7   Kiernan and Estaugh, 1993, Table 2.6.

8   Kiernan and Estaugh, 1993, Table 2.7.

9   Kiernan and Estaugh, 1993, Table 2.10.

10 Kiernan and Estaugh, 1993, Table 2.11.

11 McRae, 1993, Table 6.1, p. 90.

12 OPCS, *1991 Birth Statistics,* 1993, Tables 3.9, 3.10, 5.2.

13 For the classification see for example OPCS, *1991 Key Population and Vital Statistics,* 1993, Appendix 5.

14 The statement that race is a minor factor in English illegitimacy invariably attracts scepticism because it is so widely known that blacks, especially Caribbean blacks, have among the highest illegitimacy ratios. But race does not affect the illegitimacy ratio for England as a whole by more than a percentage point or two. The precise size of the racial effect cannot be computed directly, because the published breakdowns are based on country of birth (thus lumping together white and non-white English subjects born in England). But the decennial census publishes ethnic breakdowns by local authority, enabling at least some probes into the range of possibilities. For England and Wales as a whole 30.2 per cent of births were out of wedlock in 1991. For the subset of local authorities with at least 95 per cent whites, the ratio was 28.7 per cent—and remember that many of the small ethnic minority in those local authorities

were not blacks, with high illegitimacy ratios, but South Asians and East Asians, with very low ratios. The notion that the illegitimacy picture in England would look much different if England suddenly became all white is wrong.

15 Author's analysis of the *National Longitudinal Survey of Youth*.

16 Kiernan and Esthaugh 1993, Table 3.5; Central Statistical Office 1993, Table 5.5.

17 Smith, 1993. Older results from the *National Child Development Study* are consistent with this finding.

18 But the trend lines on joint registration are impossible to interpret for my purposes, both because they refer to the father of the new baby, not the social class from which the mother comes (a match which is especially likely to be discrepant where births out of wedlock are concerned), and because joint registration of illegitimate births is more common among the high classes than the lower ones.

19 Dennis and Erdos, 1992.

20 Dennis, 1993.

21 *The Financial Times*, 26 August 1993.

22 *The Daily Telegraph*, 8 November 1993.

23 Morgan, P., *Farewell to the Family: Public Policy and Family Breakdown in Britain and the USA*, London: IEA Health and Welfare Unit, 1995.

24 In 1991, (the most recent figures), the median before-tax weekly earnings of a full-time male worker in a manual occupation were £235.40. A quarter of all males who worked at manual occupations made £186 or less, *Central Statistical Office*, 1993, Table 6.17.

25 Kiernan and Estaugh, 1993, Table 1.3.

26 The average illegitimacy ratios for the 196 local authorities where male unemployment increased between the 1981 and 1991 censuses rose from 11.1 per cent to 27.0 per cent, an increase of 15.9 percentage points. In the 205 local authorities where male unemployment went down, the change in the illegitimacy ratio was from 10.6 per cent to 28.2 per cent, an increase of 17.6 percentage points. Overall, the correlation between change in unemployment and change in the illegitimacy ratio from 1981-91 was -.19.

27 There are other problems with treating unemployment as a cause: the unemployment rate in 1991 'predicts' illegitimacy in 1974 about as well as it 'predicts' illegitimacy in 1991. Even stranger: the 1991 unemployment figures 'predict' 1974 illegitimacy better than does the 1981 unemployment rate.

Commentaries

Back to the Future: Victorian Values for the 21st Century

Pete Alcock

Getting Worse

On his return to Britain, five years after he came to warn us of the 'bleak message' that the 'underclass' in this country, although not as substantial as in the United States, was growing rapidly, Charles Murray has, perhaps not surprisingly, discovered that in those last five years things have been getting worse. Murray was not invited over to comment that everything was 'hunky dory', and Britain has experienced a major economic recession over that period. Five years later he thus repeats his warnings, but in more apocalyptic terms, and with more pointed moral prescription.

In 1989 the problem was an 'emerging' underclass, now it is a wholesale 'British Revolution'. Last time Murray focused on *three* phenomena (causes?) associated with this—illegitimacy, violent crime and economic inactivity—now he discusses only one: *illegitimacy*. At stake, he argues, 'is the survival of free institutions and a civil society', and what is required is the restoration of the two-parent family, through marriage, as 'the norm throughout English society'. How is it that the complex, and much debated, phenomenon of the underclass (if such there be) can now be distilled into the simple problem of the changing values of matrimony? And why have these changes suddenly, at the end of the twentieth century, reached such apocalyptic proportions?

In asking, and then answering, these questions Murray's arguments become much clearer, and simpler, than they were five years ago. They also become considerably less relevant. The problem with the clearer focus is that it becomes more obvious what Murray is not talking about. And, as I shall return to later, what he is not talking about is much more important than what he is. Further, his prescriptions for future policy development thus address a much narrower portion of the social fabric. Even if they were both feasible and desirable (which, as I shall argue, they are not), they would not do much to alter many of the pressing social problems which social policy commentators and politicians in Britain (and, I had assumed, Murray himself) are most concerned about.

Whether or not they are characterised as the emergence, or establishment, of a new underclass there is now no doubt there are growing divisions within British society. Inequality is greater than it was two decades ago, and this has accentuated divisions of gender, race and age, as well as class; unemployment has remained at a consistently, and depressingly, high level; homelessness has increased; health inequalities have been widening; crime and fear of crime are rising. And yet at the same time economic performance remains, at best, sluggish; the balance of payments is deeply red; levels of taxation are rising; and government spending is being further pared back. There is no shortage of problems here for economists and social policy-makers; but Murray is concerned only about changing values on marriage and illegitimacy. In social policy terms, at least, I am afraid, such single-mindedness will not serve us well.

To be fair, we know from his previous 'warnings' that Murray's concerns for social policy were quite specifically focused. In his 1990 rejoinder, in particular, he emphasised that he was not concerned with poverty itself, but with the attitudes and responses of poor people. And poverty was not always a problem of attitudes, some poor people, for instance the frail, elderly pensioner with too little money (p. 82) should be given more money—although quite where this money should come from, given Murray's more general concern to remove any role which the state may play in public support, is not clear. Further, he recognised that evidence demonstrated that not all poor people did pass on their 'poor' values to their children. His concern was only that some did—or rather could, we can never know what they have actually done—and that more might.

The focus of Murray's concern then was on moral choices and perverse incentives. The problem of the emerging underclass was that more people were making the wrong moral choices and thus entering this class, and that welfare policies (specifically social security) were creating perverse incentives for them to do just that. In 1994 a new, and more pejorative, terminology is adopted. The underclass who are making the wrong choices are now the 'New Rabble'. And they are distinguished in moral terms from those who are making the right choices, the 'New Victorians'—or rather those who Murray *hopes* will make the right choices. For he admits that his prediction that illegitimacy rates amongst the upper middle class will in the future decrease is pure conjecture. The perverse incentives with which Murray is concerned have thus now been boiled down to the incentive for poor women to have an illegitimate child.

The 'Problem' of Illegitimacy

There was some debate, and disagreement, in 1989, in particular with Brown, (pp. 61-65) about the extent of the problem of growing rates of illegitimacy in Britain, and about the assumptions concerning family forms, and family formation, which could be made from this. Murray addresses some of these problems in 1994. As he points out, the statistics show that numbers of illegitimate births have been increasing in the past five years; and he quotes new evidence about the relatively short-lived nature of cohabiting relationships (as opposed to marriages) and tendency for such relationships to be poorer in financial and other terms. This may be true; but this evidence too could be 'sliced-up' in different ways to permit different comparisons. Short-lived or poorer relationships (married or not) could be compared on the bases of class, race, locality or age and patterns would also perhaps be revealed.

Despite the new evidence, however, Murray still does not address the points that most lone parents in Britain remain those separated or divorced (not the young mothers of illegitimate children), that most lone parents subsequently (re)marry, and that most illegitimate children are registered as living with both parents. Of course, changes are going on in family structure in Britain; and, Murray is right, levels of illegitimacy are growing. But, as the studies quoted demonstrate, these are part of broader demographic and cultural shifts, which reveal changing patterns of parenting but not necessarily a failure of it.

Even if we were to accept, however, that, all other things being equal, two parents are better at bringing up a child than one—and the research evidence quoted does not address this issue—we cannot simply use changing illegitimacy rates as a proxy measure for the absence of a father figure. And, because all those other things in practice, of course, never are equal, we cannot take either illegitimacy or the absence of a father figure as evidence that a whole range of social disasters and dislocations are being visited upon (or perpetrated by) the inhabitants of those poorer areas where illegitimacy rates are highest.

There will always be argument about what deductions can be made from statistical mapping, particularly when comparisons are made over time—and Murray is projecting back over 450 years here! We need to know whether like is being compared to like, and often it is not. And, as Murray himself concedes, statistical snapshots of populations in 1987 or 1992 cannot reveal evidence of the influence of dynamic social processes, especially those which might only recently have begun to take effect. Thus the evidence, for instance, that illegitimacy rates are higher, and growing more rapidly, in poorer local areas in Britain does not provide proof that the former is the cause of the latter—nor indeed that there is a chain of causation running in the other direction. Much more than a growth in illegitimacy is likely to be going on in these areas, and as social scientists we should know that causes are more complex phenomena than are correlations, whatever the latter may seem to reveal.

To put the same point in more simple terms we should simply consider the following non-contested (I presume) observations. Some lone parents are financially poor, indeed many are. Some live in poor neighbourhoods. Some may be less than perfect parents by one measure or another. Some children whose family was, for a time at least, comprised of a lone parent may grow up to be unemployed, to commit crime, or to bear or father an illegitimate child. But at the same time, some, arguably many, lone parent families are comprised of devoted parents and well-behaved children; while some two-parent families provide unsupportive or repressive environments for their children. And most of the unemployed, the perpetrators of crime and the cohabiting (or not) parents of illegitimate children have come from what must appear from all the evidence to be stable, married, family relationships. There are other forces at work here too.

Perverse Incentives?

In his discussion of the 'New Rabble' Murray does, however, link the growing levels of illegitimacy to other social problems such as poverty, criminality and unemployment. In particular he argues that lone parents and their children are likely to experience these problems because they become welfare dependents and lose the will to form the kind of married relationships which presumably would protect them from such risks. And lone parents become welfare dependents, not because of economic misfortune, matrimonial breakdown or exclusion from the labour market, but because of the perverse incentives contained within the benefit system which makes welfare dependency too attractive.

Many lone parents, he suggests, abuse the social security system—the implication (not a new one in right wing circles) is that somehow social security systems are there to be abused; and, if we want to stop the abuse, then perhaps we had better remove the security. However, and perhaps more importantly, he argues that even without abuse the system is too generous to lone parents, especially when compared to its treatment of married couples. This is because the couple rate of Income Support is below the rate for two individuals, and because more generous earnings rules have been introduced for lone parents to help them support themselves through paid employment. Of course, the couple rate applies to non-married, as well as married couples, and this is a rule which is on occasions quite stringently enforced to the cost of lone parents and their children. No doubt Murray would claim that it is also often abused; but this is a different point more related to his general attack on all social security.

Benefit dependency and the problem of the relative treatment of couples, individuals and lone parents are well-known issues within social security policy debate. And various proposals have been made to resolve, or restructure them. Murray suggests two 'short term' measures, which in fact would probably draw support from a wide range of political and policy opinion, at least on the left; moving to full employment and removing the benefit differential between couples and single people. It is a pity he did not explore these in a little more depth, and with a little more commitment, for they both raise important issues. But he dismisses full employment because it will not affect illegitimacy—his only concern. And he questions whether *disaggregation* (as some of the supporters of individualised benefits would call it) would be affordable in public spending terms.

More specifically, however, Murray does not just want to equalise the treatment of marriage in public policy, he wants to penalise illegitimacy. Illegitimacy was penalised economically in the past, and there was less of it then. So penalise it now, and it will decline again. To do this Murray has a disarmingly simple proposition; restore the benefit system of 1960.

Once again this demonstrates Murray's somewhat over simplistic model of social causation. If we had the benefits of 1960, then the society of 1960 would come back too. If only it would, and I could look forward to the Beatles, England winning the World Cup and the man on the moon. But it would not. History does not repeat itself. In a constantly changing world some things may appear cyclical (economic booms and recessions?), but none are repetitions. In a myriad of complex and overlapping ways social circumstances are always unique to their time. A benefit system modelled on that of 1960 might, or might not, be a policy prescription for the late 1990s, but it will not recreate 1960s values or social structures.

Actually in any case I suspect that Murray is not advocating a return to all aspects of 1960 social security policy—the insurance principle played a greater role then. His particular concern is with a means of reducing the benefits available to lone mothers in the belief that this will discourage illegitimacy—in fact not reducing them but eliminating them. Once the perverse incentives argument is accepted reduction, or removal, of benefit is the inevitable policy move, as Murray has argued before. Repeating it once again here, however, does not make it any more desirable or feasible as social policy.

It is not *desirable* because it will lead to extreme, and possibly fatal, hardship. And this hardship will not just be visited upon those whom Murray, and others, might wish morally to condemn. If all unmarried mothers, and necessarily therefore their children too, are deprived of benefits (single, separated, divorced or widowed), many good parents and deserving children, by anyone's measure, will be cruelly deprived. In a political democracy no government could realistically countenance such a move. And if an attempt were made to separate the 'deserving' parents and children from the 'undeserving' (an old theme here) then practically, and legally, the drawing of lines would be fraught with insurmountable difficulties. For instance, are divorced women to be provided for and separated women not? And, if so, what about the perverse incentives introduced there?

Basing social security policy on the presumed fear of perverse incentives is also, however, not *feasible* as social policy. This would presume that individuals make decisions about the future of their life courses based only on narrow, calculated economic gains, and that therefore they could, and should, be penalised for making the wrong choices. First year sociology students soon learn that all the decisions that we make, or think we make, are structured by a range of social, cultural and economic forces within which we move but without which we cannot step. And social policy students are taught that the purpose of policy planning can only be to aim to meet broad and predictable social needs, rather to seek to shape individual circumstances actions or desires, which will inevitably vary so widely.

Of course, all social policy is, to adopt Murray's own terminology, to some extent a form of social engineering. By providing or not providing, for people's needs we may indeed shape their behaviour. But this takes place at the level of general social and economic structures rather than individual persuasion. Murray seems to eschew such social engineering; and yet by proposing to penalise lone parents by withdrawing financial support for them and their children (where this is not available elsewhere—where it is, benefit is currently withdrawn) he is in fact recommending this in its crudest, and cruellest, form. As a prescription for social policy such individual persuasion is neither feasible nor desirable; and, thankfully, therefore, the call for it is likely to fall on deaf ears.

Victorian Values

The other side of the coin to Murray's concern with the moral degeneration of the New Rabble, is his belief in the resurrection amongst the upper middle class of a sexual Puritanism and desire for matrimony which he associates, terminologically at least, with a renewal of Victorian morality. This belief, he admits, is not based, as he claims his other predictions are, on statistical projections of recent social trends; but rather on the expectation that the opinion-forming generation which experienced the 'sexual revolution' of the 1960s and who are now in their late forties are going to be converted to religion and fidelity as their life course progresses, and are going to pass such values on to their children—who will follow these because they are true.

I shall return shortly to Murray's 'truths'. But I must admit first some surprise at the powerful role he seems to assign to the 'flower power generation'—'their remarkable power to define the *zeitgeist*' (his italics). No reason is advanced to explain why this generation, as opposed to any other before or after it, should have such a remarkable power. One might accept an assertion that all generations achieve such power as they reach their fifties, and thus begin to occupy most of the influential positions in government, commerce and media. But then the influence of this generation, for good or ill, would be, like any other, a passing phase.

As one of this cohort myself, I might be flattered to believe that we had achieved what no-one before us could, some major shift in the balance of ideological influence across the generations. But I do not. It is preposterous and self-deluding to presume that the values of any one generation can transcend, or subvert, those of others. Some people in their fifties may, as their life course develops, convert to religion or change their views on relationships; but I cannot see why this should have any more influence in the next decade than it has had in any other. Murray is confusing cohort changes with cultural changes here. Nor can I see why it is a phenomenon which will be restricted to the upper middle class, as Murray suggests. Life course changes affect all social classes. Of course in other classes other influences will be different, and perhaps Murray's perverse incentives allegations are re-entering here. But the perverse incentives would in any case apply only to those on benefits—too many people, no doubt; but not everybody outside the upper middle class.

Even if some middle-class people in their fifties do become more puritanical over the next decade, therefore, I cannot see how the argument that this will have (counter)-revolutionary social consequences can be sustained sociologically. Nor can I see how, or why, this could be championed as a return to Victorian values.

Amongst the upper middle class, Victorian family life in Britain was hierarchical and formal, rather than warm and caring; parenting was carried out largely by servants and school-masters (and mistresses); prostitution, pornography and sexual double standards were rife. Amongst the working class family life was conducted against a background of grinding poverty in which early child death took a heavy toll of both children and their mothers; older children were forced into early and unrewarding employment; and marriage rates were low by modern standards. Going back to 1960, as I have suggested, is not on—but it might have been seen as a desirable trip. Going back to the future in Victorian England would make the kind of horror story better referred to Stephen Spielberg than to John Major. Perhaps Victorian America (if that is an appropriate term) was different; but somehow I doubt it.

The 'True' Values

Murray is not, in fact, advocating a return to Victorian values, any more than he is advocating equal treatment for couples and individuals in social security, or the implementation of full employment, or more generous provision for the frail elderly. These are all tangential arguments to the main thrust of his now much clearer call to arms. Murray wants to champion marriage (presumably lifelong marriage, although he does not specify this) and to condemn illegitimacy. He calls these 'traditional' values and 'free institutions'; and he claims that they are desirable because they are 'true'.

Particularly towards the end of this most recent work on the 'British Revolution' Murray's support for traditional marriage sounds more like the preaching of a revivalist church minister than the analysis and policy prescription of an academic social scientist. To assert the truth of your own values, and consequently to dismiss all others, is a curious form of social debate. It is tactically strong, but strategically weak. Of course all who agree with you will be forced to adopt the prescriptions which you then evolve, even though they may have misgivings about some of their practical effects. But all those who do not agree can readily ignore the prescriptions by rejecting the premises; and where the prescriptions are likely to cause significant pain there is little other cause for them to give your proposals any credence.

In short Murray is asserting that it is true that marriage is always better than cohabitation or lone parenthood as a family form, and therefore it is justifiable to punish the latter forms in order to encourage the former. The evidence which he adduces in the early part of the paper does not entirely prove this assertion; but that does not matter if it is true anyway—support for marriage is an act of faith. But, if it is an act of faith, then why bother with the evidence at all? If the concern is with moral prescription, why bother with social science?

Another Agenda

In the single-minded pursuit of the devil of illegitimacy, Murray has departed in 1994 from some of the other aspects of the, alleged, problem of the emerging underclass identified in 1989, notably unemployment and criminality. And in his concern to advocate only the penalisation of unmarried mothers, he skirts over other policy recommendations concerning employment and support for couples and individuals. These are clearly no longer his primary concerns; but they are very much the concerns of others, including, I suspect, some of those who invited him back over to Britain five years on.

In the last five years Britain has experienced a major economic recession. The Prime Minister was forced to resign, by her own party. Economic policy has been subject to a series of disastrous U-turns, once within one day! Major changes in social policy in social security, health, education and social services have come into effect. Inequalities have continued to grow; and, despite government promises, taxes have been increased.

In Britain, and perhaps more interestingly in Western Europe more generally, concern has continued to develop about growing levels of poverty. These are now widely referred to as the problem of *social exclusion*—a less pejorative term than the underclass or Murray's New Rabble, although no doubt he would say 'the more's the pity'. Encapsulated in the term social exclusion is the problem of the interplay between the social and economic forces which are marginalising large groups of people who are more or less permanently outside of the labour force (including, but hardly exclusively, many lone parents) and the experience of this process by those who are the primary victims of it. It is a problem of class polarisation, of economic inactivity and disappearing opportunities, of demographic and cultural upheaval, and of the pressure to adapt social policy to meet the rapidly changing circumstances of people whose past expectations, and hopes, no longer meet their current needs.

The high levels of economic inactivity therefore require us to re-address what we mean by full employment, and how we might move forward in generating appropriate work. The growing crime rates, and even faster growing fear of them, are forcing us to debate how we might prioritise policing to best effect, how we might aim to prevent crime, and how we could better support its victims. Demographic change is requiring that we reconsider our provision for care of the elderly and infirm, and also that we ensure that children receive support where their parents are unable to provide adequately for them.

It is in this latter area that one of the most interesting of policy innovations affecting lone parents has been introduced in Britain during this period: the Child Support Agency. Given the commitment that this represents to seek to ensure that the obligations of fathers towards their children (legitimate or illegitimate), at least at a financial level, are met wherever possible, it is surprising that Murray makes no comment on it. Controversy certainly surrounds some aspects of the Agency's mission and its practice; but it is, potentially at least, a serious, and practical, attempt to enforce familial obligations, and to protect children; and there are few who object to the basic principles behind it. As a means of ensuring an improved future for the children of lone parents it is certainly a better starting point than the withdrawal of all social protection advocated by Murray, but perhaps it comes too close to condoning rather than condemnation to fit with the puritanical zeal of his new moral crusade.

As I said at the beginning, it is what Murray is not saying, rather than what he is saying, that is most significant about these comments he makes on his brief return to examine social change in Britain. He seems to have moved away from the centre stage debate about socio-economic change and social dislocation to concentrate only on a side-show performance where he preaches about the true morality of matrimony. He thus has little, or nothing, to say about the major policy developments and future policy priorities which face commentators and politicians in this country; and his prescriptions for action, directed at the false devil of illegitimacy, will I fear meet neither the challenge of practical politics nor the rigours of academic debate.

F undamentally Flawed

Miriam David

Charles Murray, as ever, writes in a fluent and intuitively readable but provocative style. However, also as ever, his arguments are fundamentally flawed in numerous respects. He lacks an appreciation, first, of the characteristics of British society, its social class structure and social and policy processes and tries to present arguments based upon the United States as if they automatically applied to Britain, without careful reconsideration. Secondly, and perhaps far more importantly, he lacks understanding of the methods of the social sciences and in particular the uses of social and economic statistics. Thus his arguments about the characteristics and consequences of the growth in the underclass are completely fallacious and misrepresented in this paper, leading to a gross form of caricature or stereotyping. In this reply I hope to demonstrate the ways in which these stereotypes have been erroneously developed through this kind of unscientific argument. Moreover, his arguments are predicated on moral rather than scientific reasoning and his politics appear to be obscured in simplistic but apparently appealing, to quote him, 'horribly sexist' sets of claims. He admits as much both at the end as well as the beginning of his essay by commenting on the changed 'public mood'.

Charles Murray argues that over the five year period since he was last in Britain there has been both an acceptance of his argument about the underclass in the public arena and a continuing growth in the underclass which indeed, according to him, substantiates his view. He does not, however, define what he means by the underclass but instead uses three 'criteria' to present his case, although this time the focus is mainly on the second and third of these. These are the growth in what he calls 'violent crime', secondly the growth in the rate of illegitimacy and thirdly in economic inactivity among what he chooses to call 'working aged men' (not, I hope, meaning elderly men in employment). He elaborates his arguments about these three trends but particularly those of births out-of-wedlock and developments in the family more generally linked to changes in unemployment. He then draws a number of policy conclusions.

In none of his arguments does he try to address the age-specific characteristics of these three trends; but attempts instead to make correlations between the gross figures of crime, illegitimacy and unemployment as if they could be seen as having causal relationships. In other words, his general argument is that these three factors together make up the underclass and, because there has been a general upward trend in each, which he shows for illegitimacy and unemployment on an area or local authority basis, this means that the argument is 'proved'. But this is to commit the Durkheimian error of correlating gross social trends with each other to prove something that might not have any kind of causal relationship. Durkheim's arguments about suicide, whilst intuitively reasonable and interesting, have on many occasions been shown to be fallacious. We simply have no evidence from the data that Murray presents as to whether or not there is a causal relationship between illegitimacy and unemployment or violent crime for that matter. Indeed it is as reasonable to argue that unemployment amongst men of working age is highest amongst the over fifties (so perhaps that is why Murray refers to them as 'working aged men') as it is to argue that illegitimacy only occurs amongst the young and teenagers, say the 15 to 24 year-olds. And although we do know that men tend to have relationships with younger women (and indeed amongst married couples two thirds of men are older than their wives) it is unlikely that the majority of these men skip a generation in choosing their partners for sexual relationships and/or procreation.

More importantly, the cornerstone of Murray's argument about the underclass is the rapid growth in illegitimacy such that, by the early 1990s, a third of all children in England and Wales are now born out-of-wedlock. This is indeed a dramatic, and perhaps staggering, figure and it certainly is worthy of consideration and explanation. However, given the fact that *one third* of births are now illegitimate, the explanation surely cannot simply be that of the underclass. Indeed if the trend continues, as Murray himself asserts that it will, it could be seen to be the *over- or majority-class* in the not too distant future. Moreover, the characteristics of this group cannot necessarily be seen as homogeneous. Again, Murray assumes that all mothers of illegitimate children are inevitably poor and/or working-class and young, even teenage. Indeed he sets out yet again on his spurious mission to 'prove' this thesis.

He begins his argument on the premise that there have been 'revolutionary' trends in the family and that the changes are new and require a new interpretation. I have absolutely no quarrel with this argument, only over the specifics of how he spells it out and the perverse policy conclusions which he ultimately draws. First his 'new interpretation' is that the changes in the family have led to a 'deterioration only in the lower class ... the upper middle class is in better shape than most people think, and it is likely to get better' (p. 102). He gets to this assertion by rather dubious and indeed circuitous means covering illegitimacy, divorce, cohabitation and social class. He starts off by delving far back into history and using ecclesiastical records to demonstrate the trends in illegitimacy. However, it is extremely difficult to compare ecclesiastical data with census or other social statistics data collected by 'modern' means. And indeed, social and family historians are forever quarrelling about the meanings and significance to be attached to such different forms of evidence. Even if Murray's argument is only intended to be journalistic rather than real scholarship, it is simply sloppy not to acknowledge the difficulties in these kinds of comparison and interpretation.

His second set of arguments about the changes in the family relates to trends in divorce and cohabitation. Again he asserts that the growing trend towards divorce 'proves' that marriage is now less meaningful than it used to be. This is indeed a curious interpretation of the nature of 'meaningfulness'. In fact, sociologists and family historians across the social and political spectrum have drawn a variety of conclusions about these trends. For example, one of the most famous in Britain, Ronald Fletcher, argues that the trends in divorce and remarriage demonstrate the continuing popularity of marriage as an institution and indeed he also shows how the rates of marriage and remarriage have never been higher.[1] Similarly, but from a completely different perspective, Delphy and Leonard argue that, despite the changing rates of divorce, marriage remains a key institution of family life in capitalism, drawing their examples from both Britain and France today.[2]

Murray also uses flimsy evidence about cohabitation to assert that marriage is now less 'meaningful'. He admits that the trends in cohabitation, however, also show that three-quarters of all illegitimate births are registered in the names of both parents who are also living at the same address. This leads him to the 'conclusion' that 70 per cent of children live with married couples, 16 per cent with unmarried couples and 14 per cent with women living alone. He also links the trends in cohabitation to social policy and erroneously assumes that all such families, in other words lone mother families, are in receipt of social welfare benefits. He does not seem to be aware that the cohabitation rule is alive and well in Britain in the 1990s just as it was in the 1970s, even though its form may have altered to be slightly less draconian in terms of snoopers!

The supposed strength of Murray's case about the revolutionary trends in the family lies in his arguments about modernity and social class and his attempt to add flesh to this by analysing small area statistics comparing trends in unemployment and illegitimacy. He focuses upon 10 'rich' or upper-middle-class and 10 lower-working-class or 'poor' areas. He then pinpoints two contrasting local authorities for detailed analysis, namely Middlesbrough as an example of a 'lower-working-class' community versus Wokingham as an 'upper-middle-class' community. He sees Wokingham as an example of a community of what he describes as 'new Victorians' and Middlesbrough as an example of a community which he chooses to depict as the 'New Rabble'. The former is one of the two-parent family type 'in good shape' whereas the latter is a prime example of a community using an entirely different 'social template' and full of illegitimate children living alone with their mothers. I must say that I personally am relieved to find that I do not live in either of these two communities with such pejorative depictions and which bear so little resemblance to the social scientific literature about communities in Britain today.

Having sketched in these two contrasting communities Murray extrapolates to the 'individual' case and asserts that this will produce a dramatically changed class structure, bifurcated into the upper middle class and lower working class each characterised by their family structure such that the two-parent family is the essence for the upper middle class and illegitimacy that for the lower working class. Whilst it would be difficult to quarrel with the view that in the late twentieth century in Britain, as in other advanced industrial societies, there are dramatic changes occurring to the class structure it is unlikely to be as simplistic as Murray would like to paint it and have us believe. And his characterisation of the upper middle class as the New Victorians is rather far-fetched as is the attribution of the lone parent families as part of, or even all of, the 'New Rabble'. Both are deeply insulting to the members of these social groups whether they are new or not.

Even more of an insulting caricature is the example he draws of members of the 'New Rabble' claiming social benefits. He present us with the fictitious character of Scully who is quite simply a 'rogue extraordinaire', falsely claiming housing and other social benefits etc. Oddly the character is a *male* and it is not at all clear who his partner is and whether or not he cohabits. Presumably the example is meant to show an unemployed man, scrounging off both his lone parent partner and the welfare state and, by implication, compelled to do so by having grown up in a lone mother household with no father role model on which to rely! All this leads Murray to his overly dramatised critique of the British system of income maintenance and social welfare. He does, however, seem to feel that in this respect the chief problem is unemployment not illegitimacy.

In his confusion, therefore, he presents us with both a critique of current systems of welfare and social security and of the two main political parties. For example, he even suggests difficulties for the Labour Party as the party of the lower working class and therefore single parents or all those with illegitimate children and the Tories as that of the Wokinghams of this world. In other words, the Tories only represent the two-parent families 'who are in good shape'. This is hardly consonant with the antics of some Tory MPs to whom he even alludes.

Nevertheless, his conclusions, although muddled, are strong and morally self-righteous. He adopts the Labour Party plea for stronger policies on employment but on the grounds that if men had jobs they would be able to support their wives and children. Hence his other proposal is that women be 'persuaded' only to have children in a proper marital situation where they can be supported by their husbands (and so not go out to work, I presume!). This idea that men need families to civilise them and to 'force' them to do their patriarchal duty is ages old. A decade ago, a compatriot of Murray's, George Gilder, suggested that 'men had been cuckolded by the compassionate state' and he too recommended a social policy, to the

Reagan administration, that would also aim to discourage women from having children out-of-wedlock.[3] In the 1930s in England similar social policies were also proposed although perhaps in more muted and less sexist language. These policies have been tried and tested and found wanting. It simply will not do to keep harping on about the past and the 'Golden Age' of the family. Was it really ever thus? And even if it were, why has it changed? Is it simply because women are perverse or is it because men do need to think more clearly and carefully about what they want and what is in fact possible for men and women alone and together in late twentieth century Britain or the USA? Such questions are social and cannot be answered by the sort of commentary, rather than analysis, that Murray provides.

Notes

1   Fletcher, R., *The Shaking of the Foundations: Family and Society*, London: Routledge, 1988.

2   Delphy, C. and Leonard, D., *Familiar Exploitation*, Cambridge: Polity Press, 1992.

3   Gilder, G., *Wealth and Poverty*, New York: Basic Books, 1981.

W here are the New Victorians?

Melanie Phillips

Charles Murray is like a bit of chewing gum that gets stuck to the sole of your shoe. You scrape it off in disgust, but your shoe still sticks to the pavement as you walk. When you remove the shoe and peel off the remainder of the offending gum, you find the sole comes away in your hands. It was rotten anyway. It was all too vulnerable to attack.

It is impossible to shake off Murray's analysis of Britain's underclass because it has exposed a decay at the core of our society that most of us would prefer to ignore. Reactions to Murray, among those who are politically of the centre or of the left, are violent and troubled. There are those who dismiss him as unspeakably vile, for whom his name will never pass their lips except as an expletive, who denounce the very word 'underclass' as an anathema never to be used in civilised society. For them, the situation of our poorest communities, their lifestyle, behaviour and attitudes are largely to be accepted without adverse comment. And where some blame is clearly called for, any such criticism must be laid squarely at the door of the government for reducing these communities to this plight.

But there are others, of whom I am one, no less opposed to Conservative politics, who are fascinated and repelled by Murray's analysis in almost equal measure. For us, he has drawn attention to an alarming social development which cannot wholly be explained away as the outcome of economic circumstances. We recognise that this is a cultural phenomenon which owes as much to egalitarian social individualism as to the brutalities of the free market. But at the same time we recoil from the selective nature of his analysis, not to mention his scorched earth solution.

Like Murray, I believe that the progressive collapse of the intact family is bringing about a set of social changes which is taking us into uncharted and terrifying waters. Like Murray, I recognise that there are now whole communities, framed by structural unemployment, in which fatherlessness has become the norm. These communities are truly alarming because children are being brought up with dysfunctional and often antisocial attitudes as a direct result of the fragmentation and emotional chaos of households in which sexual libertarianism provides a stream of transient and unattached men servicing their mothers. But, unlike Murray, I do not believe that the collapse of the intact family is confined to the lower social classes. I do not believe that it has been caused by the welfare state. And I most certainly do not believe that the solution is effectively to starve poor women and children back into marriage.

The collapse of the family may take different forms in different social classes, but its roots and its effects are the same. Fragmented families cause children hardship and disadvantage. Relatively speaking, children whose families are no longer intact do worse in virtually every area of life than children from intact families, looked after throughout their childhood by their own father and mother. That holds true for middle-class children as much as for children from lower social classes. Children's problems are by no means confined to those brought up by single parents. Step-parents often create worse problems. The distress and damage done to a middle-class child shunted around between step-households may take the form of depression, eating disorders, educational under-achievement and an inability to form lasting adult relationships; they are no less destructive than the effects on the lower-class child who may truant, sniff glue and drift into crime.

The accelerating rates of divorce, cohabitation and out-of-wedlock births are being driven along by the revolution in women's expectations and economic circumstances. And while it is obviously the case, as Murray suggests, that middle-class women have been economically liberated through employment while women at the bottom of the pile have been economically freed by welfare benefits, it is perverse to target attention and blame on those lower-class women. Our whole culture has devalued marriage to a breakable contract of little intrinsic worth, and children to merely another set of consumer commodities. We have created a society in which children are increasingly expected to satisfy adult rights to individual fulfilment, rather than be the repository of adult duties and responsibilities.

Advances in embryology are underscoring this new and amoral attitude towards children. Their best interests are being discarded along a line of family dismemberment which leads all the way from virgin births to serial partners. From self-impregnation courtesy of the local sperm bank to multiple monogamy, fathers are increasingly participating in the family, in A.H. Halsey's pungent phrase, as no more than a genital. Popular culture overwhelmingly proclaims these messages. As I write, current issues of women's magazines promise: 'Why men walk out; three men who left their partner' and 'My wife and mistress are both pregnant', *Marie-Claire*; 'Sex and the single girl; when he decides it's over', *Cosmopolitan*; 'When sex is brilliant but the relationship stinks', *19*. Every day, every week, every month, magazines, films, TV, popular music, tabloid and so-called quality newspapers, all conform to the same cultural expectations.

Clearly, it is not welfare that's created these new social norms. Yet Murray not only draws on statistical evidence to support such an analysis, but goes even further to suggest that while the lower orders are all breeding like illegitimate rabbits, the middle classes are rediscovering marriage, fidelity and responsibility. Hence his division of British society into the New Victorians and the New Rabble. This is not merely viciously offensive but it is bunk. Murray's trick is to put sets of statistics side by side and then extrapolate from them theories of cause and effect. Not surprisingly, they don't stand up to scrutiny. The situation is much more complex. As he himself concedes, his prediction of New Victorianism is just that, 'pure prediction, not an extrapolation from existing trends'. He adduces not a shred of evidence to support this prediction; not surprisingly, because the trends are going in the opposite direction.

According to the OPCS *Birth Statistics 1992*, since the beginning of the 1980s jointly registered births outside marriage increased three to four fold for *each* social class. And the greatest increase was in Classes I and II. So much for the New Victorians. Murray makes much of the fact that more illegitimate babies are being born to the lower social classes. But again the facts are more complex. The lower classes have more babies. According to the 1991 Census, there were 1,756,093 people in Social Classes IV and V and the skilled manual class, compared to 1,849,893 people in Classes I and II and the skilled non-manual class. But although there were nearly 100,000 fewer of them, the lower social group gave birth to more babies: 336,000 compared to 258,000. According to these figures, Social Classes IV and V produce more babies proportionate to their numbers than Classes I and II. Moreover, so far from being a rabble it is the skilled working-class that produces the most jointly registered births outside marriage. And it is that very same social class that turns out to be producing the most children *inside* marriage as well.

Murray's statistics, therefore, are selective and misleading. They are selected to back up his theory that lower-working-class illegitimacy is the problem. The question has to be asked why he concentrates so heavily on this selective interpretation at the expense of a more comprehensive and accurate, if more complex, analysis. It is hard to ignore the fact that Murray himself is divorced and has fathered children in two households. What appears to be acceptable behaviour for himself, a middle-class man who can afford to maintain such a lifestyle, is to be condemned among those who are less well-heeled. Maybe therefore it's not surprising that divorce hardly figures in Murray's social apocalypse. Yet all the evidence suggests that for many children it is the end of their world.

The collapse of the intact family is a social disaster. It weakens the cultural and moral transmitters down through the generations. It lies at the heart of many of our social problems. Personally, I believe that if we are unable to check it we will produce a society dangerously divided not along social class lines, as Murray suggests, but *within* each class. The barricades will go up between intact families whose members prosper and who can form constructive civic bonds and fractured families whose members are desperately disadvantaged and who cannot connect and form constructive communities.

We may not be able to do anything about this. Maybe, as many suggest, these new social patterns are irreversible. But if we are going to have any chance of halting our slide over the social precipice, we're not going to achieve it by treating part of our society as alien, a race apart, a rabble. We are one society. These cultural developments run through it as a fault line from top to bottom. So any remedy has to be comprehensive and fair, not divisive and vindictive. If the plant is once again to bloom, it is the roots that have to be treated. We shouldn't just chop off some of the leaves.

I believe that there are serious limits to what the state can do to change people's behaviour. People will only change the way in which they live if they are convinced that it is in their interests and the interests of their society for them to do so, and that the social consequences of not doing so are too severe to be tolerated. Intellectuals and politicians therefore bear an enormous responsibility to stop peddling the silly lie that the dismembered family is no worse than the intact family. And the middle classes bear a heavy responsibility too to re-affirm *by their own behaviour* the desirability of bringing up children inside a stable marriage. How the middle classes behave has huge resonance for classes lower down the social scale, since it is the middle classes to which they aspire and whose lifestyle they wish to share.

But however limited the role of the state may be, it does play some part in this process. At present, for example, the tax and benefits systems produce some perverse anti-marriage effects. These should be reversed, not merely because economic circumstances play *some* part in determining people's lifestyles but because law and public policy have a significant declaratory effect which should not be underestimated. They help announce the moral standards a society thinks are desirable. The dilemma, however, is producing a political and economic culture that actively favours marriage which does not in its train punish the children in dismembered families and make their predicament even worse than it already is.

Our society does not at present publicly declare itself in favour of marriage; quite the opposite. We must do so, while finding a way through the dilemma to protect *all* children. This means not cutting off all welfare benefits to single mothers, but offering more carrot than stick to make marriage the attractive option. At the same time, the declaratory route should mean that divorce should not be made easier and assisted fertility should only be provided for married couples. It is probably the middle classes who would scream loudest at such unequivocal support for marriage. That is the measure of the problem we face. It is also the measure of the vindictive irrelevance of any solution that merely targets the poor.

W ould You take One Home with You?

Sue Slipman

Our century has plotted its course through the growth of individual rights. This process accelerated in the 1960s and when, in the 1980s, the libertarian free marketeers broke the post-war consensus, they broke up our traditional social framework of inter-locking obligations. All these changes happened within a period of massive economic, industrial and technological change. The 1990s have given rise to the growth of a breed of moral panickers who are alarmed at the changes wrought within the social fabric and in particular within the institution of the family and who now wish to re-assert a new agenda that is based on duties not rights. The problem they face is that the last twenty years and more have taken society's lid off the box. The force required to shove it firmly back on requires a methodology that it is totally out of sync with our secular, pluralist humanitarian democracy.

I do not wish to be entirely churlish to the alarmists. There are some grounds for agreement. We clearly need to take stock of social change and recognise that the combination of factors causing change risk creating a social order in which greed and easy self-fulfilment become the norm. I agree with Charles Murray that there are new values in gestation and that some of them will be welcome. They include trustworthiness, and meeting the duties that responsibility for others confers upon you. But we will not, I hope, move back to an outmoded hypocrisy that denies human freedom and growth.

Unlike the panickers I do not believe that all the changes over these twenty years have been deleterious. Some changes have brought positive good and have developed a story that has taken as long as the century to unfold. I am hopeful that we can incorporate the positive changes over these years whilst we address their downside. We could move on to a new order in which rights and duties balance each other and in which human freedoms will be exercised alongside human responsibilities.

The Victorian family that now delights Murray and others hid the powerlessness of women and children as property within the family.

It is true that the family as male property has been the traditional method of socialising and containing the warrior in man, but the twentieth century has been a battle for women and children to have rights of their own within the structure of the family in a way that has encroached upon the power of men. They can now in theory negotiate with men, but the family has become an arena of conflict in which individuals fight for enough space, power and share in the resources they need to sustain them.

The moral panickers demonise the one-parent family but it is more accurately and properly understood as a result of the modern conflict within the two-parent family, coupled with the process of sharp industrial and economic change. Lone parenthood is the result of major societal changes—not their cause.

Lone parents are not a breed apart. They hold the same moral values as everyone else. They want the same access to success for their children and they are as prepared as all other parents to take responsibility for them. Indeed if they did not do so on a day-to-day basis our social problems would be a lot more pressing than they are. Moreover most lone parents would give their eye teeth for a decent relationship with a partner to support them in parenting. Few chose to be lone parents.

Murray's analysis concentrates on the rate of births outside marriage. But the majority of lone parents on benefit are mature men and women who have been married. He also dismisses the dramatic rise in cohabitation as having no real significance in mitigating the numbers. The truth is that we do not know how many never married lone parents have been cohabiting—but the indications are that a fair number believed they were in a stable partnership.

Murray takes the period of Victorian industrialisation and argues that if rapid change and modernity were the cause of lone parenthood it would have been seen in this era, but in fact the rate of non-marital children declined. What he fails to take into account is that the rise of the factory and manufacturing industries created large numbers of jobs that paid for marriages and sustained families. The technological era is vastly different. The industrial revolution ushered in the age of trades union aspirations for the family wage. We now live in an age when income from wages for many families needs supplementing from the benefit system. Part-time jobs in McDonalds cannot provide like full-time manufacturing jobs.

Certainly the unskilled manual working class are producing less stable unions between men and women. It is here that the traditional nuclear family is under most pressure. In the nuclear family men were the breadwinners and women the childrearers. The death of the staple industries killed off the family form and the communities that were once sustained by the family wage earned by the male. There are no more mothers than there have ever been in these communities; there are just fewer committed fathers.

Men in Social Class V are unlikely ever again to be breadwinners. Murray argues that full employment is part of the solution, but he acknowledges that this will not by itself ensure that women will be prepared to marry men. But even if a return to full employment on the traditional model is the desirable solution—it is not going to happen. The new jobs coming on stream are better suited to the working patterns and skills of women rather than men. This has produced a challenge to male identity. The traditional routes for men into adulthood of wage earning and authority figure in the family are no longer open. They have lost their traditional role but they have not found another one that would make them attractive to women. The resulting conflict between men and women has lead to an increase in domestic violence over these years of change: a phenomenon that Murray dismisses as insignificant. Our police thankfully take it more seriously.

Accompanying changes to the industrial structure has been the rise of female ambition. Most women now work. They are less willing to accept a subservient role within the family than they once were when dependent upon male industry for an income. But most women still want to have children and, from what we can tell, most still aspire to a decent relationship with a partner as the best way of bringing up those children. Very few women chose lone parenthood. Most of those who do are middle-class, professional women who can usually afford the costs of their child. If there is a new model for relationships between men and women it will be based on partnership where both partners have to work towards acquiring family income —and in many cases they will need ongoing subsidy from the state to tackle in-work poverty.

Men and women in higher social classes are more likely to achieve positive partnerships as parents. They have far more affluence to lose in breaking their relationships than do those lower down the social scale. Dual-earner couples enjoy very affluent life styles. Domestic responsibilities continue to fall more heavily upon women regardless of their work patterns. But, high income couples can pay someone else to do their cleaning and look after their children, allowing both partners enough freedom. They do not have to confront the conflict between their freedom as individuals and being left holding the baby.

As you move down the social class structure these pressures upon the combining of roles of parent and worker become more obvious. In Social Class V both roles now fall more heavily upon women, men having largely absented themselves from the process. Increasingly if men have little to bring to the family party and women continue to sustain the burden of parenting and breadwinning—they will go on questioning what is the point of a man.

Murray argues that rising crime is directly connected to all these facets. It stands to reason that it is infinitely harder to bring up a child alone and to provide resources than it is to do so with a committed partner. Indeed most lone parents live on the poverty line with few resources. You would expect to find a higher incidence of delinquent activity from children in one- than two-parent families, and you do. It is nine per cent for two-parent families and 16 per cent for one-parent families. But most of this crime is petty juvenile misbehaviour—not serious crime—and more importantly you cannot base a public policy on the fact that 84 per cent of lone parents are doing a good job in bringing up their children.

It is true that what is happening to our young men is very worrying. It appears that as the traditional routes into adulthood no longer exist for them, many have removed themselves from any concept of parental responsibility. Increasingly when the sex that they see as purely recreational becomes procreation they react as if they had no role in the process. I would be a rich woman if I had a pound for every time I have heard a man talk about 'these girls who make themselves pregnant'.

I have no doubt that removal of men from parenting is extremely bad for their development as civilised human beings. They are being infantilised and there is a crisis in male identity. But any discussion about the family which is gender neutral will inevitably get it wrong. Furthermore any discussion about the family which does not call for men to change, or for wealth and power to be more fairly distributed between family members, necessarily wishes to return traditional power and authority to men.

So, it comes as no surprise that Murray's radical solutions are to punish women and children back into dependence upon men. He would starve them back into such dependence. But if men cannot meet that dependence through work there is no point in doing this apart from trying to make the working class behave more like the middle class, to curb the power of uppity women and to stop the lower orders from breeding excessively. Eugenicists have been trying to do that from time immemorial.

Murray is right that the benefit system allows women and children to survive without men, but it is not the cause of the breakdown in relations between men and women. It is not only more humane, it also makes better sense to assist lone parents to economic independence, whilst we find better strategies to socialise men to accept power sharing and responsibility with women.

I have no doubt that such a strategy involves a new consensus around parental responsibility based on an acceptance that the child has rights and parents have duties regardless of their marital relationship. This consensus has to be shored up by a successful operation on the part of the Child Support Agency ensuring that all parents at least fulfil the basic duty of maintaining their child.

The values of parental responsibility have to be taught in our schools alongside sex education and a new emotional literacy amongst young men. We need a positive programme to prevent teenage parenthood by enhancing the self esteem of the young to make them less likely to succumb to peer group pressure for early sexual activity for which they may not be emotionally equipped. Ensuring that girls leave school with qualifications and job prospects would be recognition that all too many will be left holding the baby.

We will also need programmes of support to enable young parents to be competent parents. Helping all lone parents to work so that they build their self esteem and give their children a stable working pattern to aspire to as well as cutting costs to the taxpayer may be crucial. But forcing them to work full time so that they cannot supervise their adolescent children may be a disaster.

Cutting state benefits for mothers will make our problems worse, not better. The divorced or separated mother is in exactly the same financial position as the never married mother under our system. Charles Murray's prescription will simply ensure that, regardless of their route into lone parenthood, mothers and children will not survive. He openly admits that he has a misogynist agenda ('It is all horribly sexist I know') but he still cannot explain why any woman in her right mind should want to take one of his new rabble home with her.

Statistical Update

Alan Buckingham

It is more than six years since Charles Murray first intervened in the British underclass debate. Many of his claims and predictions were dismissed at the time either on the basis of a lack of quality evidence or his lack of familiarity with British society. In this appendix I shall update Murray's data using official statistics, outline recent developments in the debate over the underclass in Britain, and draw on my own analysis of the National Child Development Study to help us adjudicate between some of the competing claims.

Statistics

Lone-parenthood and Illegitimacy

Since 1961 there has been a four-fold increase in the proportion of dependent children living in one-parent families. Lone-parent families with dependent children now account for over a fifth of all families with dependent children. This proportion rises to nearly a third in the North West of England, or if we divide by ethnic group the proportion for Afro-Caribbeans reaches 45 per cent. As a result, by 1993 an estimated 2.3 million dependent children were living in lone-parent families in Great Britain. Of these lone parents, single never-married mothers are now the largest single component (Figure 1, p. 176), which, in turn, is due to a seven-fold increase in the number of single never-married mothers between 1971 and 1992, compared with a three-fold increase for divorced and separated mothers.[1]

The continuous rise in the number of lone parents has its origin in the increasing number of births outside marriage, the falling marriage rate and the increasing number of couples divorcing. So, one might be reassured by recent data (Figure 2, p. 176) showing that the raw number of live births born out of wedlock peaked in 1993. At the same time as Murray was writing *Underclass: The Crisis Deepens* (in 1994) the total dropped for the first time since 1976, and from the provisional figures for 1995 this pattern may be repeated. Despite this, the relative measure of illegitimacy, that is the *percentage* of live births outside of marriage, indicates a continued increase.[2] The apparent paradox can be accounted for by the sharp drop in the total number of live births to all women that began in 1991. So while there are fewer illegitimate babies being born than in 1993, a greater proportion of babies are being born into lone parent families than since records began.

Meanwhile, by 1993 the marriage rate had dropped to its lowest level in more than one hundred and fifty years, and the numbers divorcing had increased nearly seven-fold between the 1960s and the 1990s to the point where only a few thousand fewer divorces than first marriages took place in 1993.[3] Taken as a whole, the trends originally described by Murray show no signs of reversing.

Which Class is Responsible for the Trends?

The problem with national trends such as the ones just described is that they are probably masking differing trends between classes, and crucial to Murray's thesis is such a claim; rather than illegitimacy being spread evenly across all social groups, *it is the underclass who are disproportionately responsible for these births, and their behaviour is increasingly discordant with the rest of society.* In support of this, in both *The Emerging British Underclass* and *Underclass: The Crisis Deepens* Murray found large and growing differences in the illegitimacy rate between local authorities with the fewest and most Class V households. Figure 3, (p. 177) adds another three years to his graph on p. 130. While the rate of increase of illegitimacy has slowed from 1990 onwards for both sets of local authority areas, the slow down has been greater for the areas with fewest Class V households.

The evidence Murray provides is, however, hardly conclusive proof that it is the lower working class who are the main perpetrators of illegitimate births. Dealing with data at the local authority level is (as Murray himself recognises) far from satisfactory, for we cannot extrapolate from aggregate trends to individual behaviours. For example, an increase in illegitimate births in an area with a large proportion of Class V individuals does not necessarily indicate that it is the Class V people who are having the illegitimate children. What is really needed to test out Murray's thesis is data at the level of individuals, and Melanie Phillips has provided this.[4] She shows that, since the 1980s, the fastest proportionate increase in jointly registered births outside marriage has, in fact, occurred in classes I and II and the largest number of jointly registered births occurred in the skilled manual class. On this evidence illegitimacy is not just a lower working class problem.

Closer analysis of the data, however, does not support Phillips conclusion.[5] A large proportion of the increase in the numbers of illegitimate babies born to the middle class (classes I and II) can be explained by the rapid increase in the size of the class in recent years; if more people are in a class then we expect more babies from that class, illegitimate or not. Meanwhile, there has been a sharp reduction in the number of men entering the working class (classes IV and V), so here we would expect a reduction in the raw number of all births.[6]

Once we take into account these structural changes, both the middle class and working class have had an equally dramatic increase in the number of illegitimate births, equating to a near three-fold increase between 1983 and 1993. Moreover, these figures hide the fact that the rapid increase for the middle class was from a very low base, and that by 1993 (the last available year) the rate of increase for the middle class may be levelling off unlike the rate for the working class (see Figure 4, p. 178). Finally, it is not the skilled manual class that is over-represented in the ranks of the illegitimate parents as Phillips claims, but Class IV and V parents. Table 1 (p. 175) shows this by comparing the numbers of illegitimate births we would expect if these births were spread evenly according to the size of each class, with the real number of illegitimate births.[7] Overall the gap in the illegitimacy rate during the 1990s has grown between the classes, as Murray predicted, offering general support for Murray's 'second scenario' postulated in *Underclass: The Crisis Deepens*, that the swelling illegitimacy ratio will be largely confined to the lower working class.

Unemployment and Labour Market Inactivity

In *The Emerging British Underclass* Murray says proof that an underclass has arrived can be seen when 'large numbers of young, healthy, low-income males choose not to take jobs' (p. 37). If long-term unemployment is one indicator of this then the drop in the absolute number of long-term male unemployed from a peak of 925,000 in 1993 to just under 800,000 by spring 1995 is promising.[8] In spite of this, there is mounting evidence of a growing population of men who have become detached from the experience of work. First, the drop in the numbers of long-term unemployed was not as rapid as the overall drop in the numbers unemployed, and second, the percentage of hardened unemployed, those out of work for more than three years, *increased* from 14.5 per cent to 21 per cent of all unemployed men.

This last statistic cannot be explained by older men giving up their search for work as they near retirement, for there was a 5 per cent drop in the number of men over 50 years of age making up the hardened unemployed, while for young men, between 20 and 29 years of age, there was a one third *increase*. In short, we are witnessing a growing proportion of young men who cannot or will not work, seemingly regardless of economic conditions.

Current Debates

Are State Benefits or Cultural Changes Responsible for the Growth in the Underclass?

The debate in the US over the cause of the underclass has swung from explanations based on the direct economic incentives of the welfare system, inducing people to become welfare dependent, to cultural explanations arguing that the value of the welfare package is less relevant than the message it conveys to poor people about their behaviour. Recently, social scientists have begun to pin the blame for the growth of the underclass on a broader decline in morality and reduction in individual responsibility across the whole of society.

Murray implicates both 'economic' and 'cultural' theories in his explanation for the growth of the underclass. State benefits are the starting point in the creation of the underclass, luring people into dependency, offering short-term gains (e.g. freedom from the 'drudgery' of work), at the expense of long-term losses (e.g. failure to gain precious work skills). The behaviour becomes self-defeating over time as those dependent on welfare benefits lose the personal discipline and esteem work brings, become unemployable and eventually slump into a fatalistic culture.

Once this behaviour has taken root Murray does not think that simply by reducing benefit levels the size of the underclass will be reduced. The culture of the underclass, the attitude of fatalism and an unwillingness to think ahead, radiates outwards across generations and through neighbourhoods, drawing people into the underclass who would not have been enticed by the economic incentives of welfare benefits alone. Reinforcing this, the act of providing guaranteed benefits and housing to lone mothers sends a moral message to the poor, declaring that it is fine to act in an irresponsible manner since the state will pick up the tab. Eventually, as lone-parenthood and welfare dependency becomes the norm in housing estates, the social stigma attaching to such behaviour weakens. And so, the final barrier to a mass underclass vanishes.

Murray's theory has been criticised by some social scientists because it is said to underplay the causal role changes in the moral climate across *all* social groups have had in the creation and growth of the underclass.[9] Mainstream culture has, over the last thirty years, turned on its head the moral values of hard work, sex within marriage and the essential equity of capitalism preferring instead personal permissiveness and system blaming. The responsibility for these changes lies with the libertarian collectivist élite who, in attempting to 'liberate' themselves, have shaped mainstream culture to accept similar values.

Although perhaps liberating for the élite, the same values are disastrous for the poor since it traps them in poverty. A value system that favours moral relativism while holding in disdain an 'unegalitarian' society conveys the message to those who work in low paying 'dead-end' jobs that they are 'fools', while the underclass are 'victims' of an unjust system. If there is no respect or honour to be gained from sustaining a family on a low wage, and those around you not in work are thought to be there due to circumstances beyond their control, then why bother acting in a responsible manner?

The counterview is that welfare benefits are the underlying cause of welfare dependence and the change in dominant ideas. Temporally, such a thesis fits the facts better. Each major change in the benefit system appears to be followed by a corresponding change in some individuals' behaviour. Crime rates began to rise in the 1950s, ten years after universal state welfare was established. Lone-parenthood increased rapidly during the 1970s, shortly after increases in the value and breadth of benefits to lone parents made living without a partner financially feasible. Finally, the three-fold increase in the number of men leaving the labour force and registering as disabled since the late 1970s is, according to the economists Nickell and Bell, associated with the increasing ease with which invalidity benefit has become available.[10]

Is Poverty or Family Structure the Cause of Childhood Academic Failure?

There is a strong association between relative poverty and lone-parenthood mainly because nine out of ten single mothers are at any one time in receipt of Income Support.[11] So evidence that children from these backgrounds do less well academically is frequently claimed to be the result of poverty, and not single or lone-parenthood as Murray would claim. Patricia Morgan's book *Farewell to the Family?* represents the most sophisticated critique of those who argue poverty is the cause.[12] Summarising a variety of British and American studies on lone-parenthood she shows that, controlling for income, boys from lone-parent backgrounds do worse,[13] and the cause lying behind this is lack of a father.[14] British longitudinal studies clearly show that children of lone parents were significantly more likely to leave school early and that most of those in the study who had done well by the age of 23 had come from an intact and never-broken two parent family.[15] Many who accept this evidence, revert instead to the position that, since *some* children from two parent families do less well than *some* children from lone-parent families, the notion that lone parenthood is the cause of childhood failure must be wrong. But as Dennis and Erdos have pointed out, as with all social science, we are looking at averages or patterns in a selected sample.[16] Finding one excellent lone parent does not falsify the claim that, on average, children do better in a married family.

Analysing the Underclass

A strong theme in the resistance to Murray's work has been an objection to the explanatory weight he places on individual causes of the underclass rather than structural-economic causes. Murray's view is of an underclass made up of individuals with deplorable attitudes who lack foresight. The counter view sees the underclass as unlucky members of the working-class who have been made victims by economic circumstances.[17] Is Murray right? Are the underclass partly responsible for their own predicament?

My analysis here is based on a definition of the underclass as 'chronic state dependants' and compares them to the rest of the working-class.[18] The National Child Development Study (NCDS) is the basis of the analysis. It is a survey which has followed all children born during one week in 1958, revisiting them five times, the last visit being in 1991 when the members in the sample were 33 years old. The data set is rare in that, instead of a snap-shot view of the population at one point in time, we have a detailed history of each individual. We now can begin to answer causal questions because we can place the order of events, for example whether low work motivation was the *result* of loss of work or the *cause* of it.

Are the Underclass Workshy?

In *The Emerging British Underclass* Murray provides anecdotal evidence in support of his claim that there exists an underclass of men indifferent to work. In contrast, current academic evidence indicates that work commitment among the underclass is high and that weak attachment to the labour market can instead be explained by lack of unskilled secure jobs.[19] Who is right?

The NCDS sample were asked their opinions on a number of statements, two of which represent good measures of work commitment. The first was 'I would pack in a job I didn't like even if there was no job to go to'. The second was 'Almost any job is better than none'. Tables 2a and 2b (p. 175) show the difference of opinion between underclass men and working-class men, revealing the underclass to be much less committed to work.

Going back to their childhood years, we find the underclass were likely to have had significantly more time absent from school compared with the working class and were significantly more likely to be rated apathetic by their teachers. When asked about their aspirations at age 16 the underclass were significantly less likely to want to stay on to study and more likely to say they 'didn't know' what they wanted to do. So at an early age these boys showed a lack of interest in work that they were later to exhibit in adulthood, confirming that part of the reason for their current predicament lies with their own lack of motivation.

Underlying the differences between the underclass and the rest of the NCDS sample are inherited differences in cognitive ability, something that Murray does not discuss in his two books on the underclass but is the central theme of *The Bell Curve*. Even when compared with the below average scoring working class, the underclass are significantly less intelligent.[20]

Looking at lone-parenthood amongst underclass females, further support for the important role of cognitive ability is obtained. Kiernan's study, also using NCDS data, found that if a girl's educational attainment was in the lowest quartile she was nearly seven times more likely to become a teenage mother than if her attainment was in the upper quartile.[21] Kiernan's finding lead her to conclude that improved investment in education may be a crucial component in preventing early parenthood. However, much of the educational 'attainment' score may be the result of innate cognitive ability rather than the result of the educational system. This can be supported on two grounds; Table 3 (p .175) shows the mean ability level at age 11 of women below 24 years of age, comparing all in the NCDS sample who married before the child's birth with those members of the underclass unmarried before the child's birth. The ten point difference in the score (out of 80) suggests a highly significant difference in ability. The second ground for support comes from Murray's own work. In *The Bell Curve* Herrnstein and Murray note that although intelligence in itself cannot explain the explosion in illegitimacy, there is 'a direct and strong relationship between ... low intelligence and the likelihood that the child will be born out of wedlock'.[22] They hypothesise that the relationship exists because less intelligent women are less likely to think ahead, to think in advance about birth control or consider a wise time to have a child.

It is important to make clear that Murray and Herrnstein are not claiming that we can 'read off' from an individual's cognitive ability whether they are going to be part of the underclass or not. Low intelligence is perhaps a necessary, but certainly not a sufficient condition for underclass membership. The vast majority of the poor with little cognitive ability are still able to be admirable citizens because avoiding welfare dependence and staying married has much to do with personal qualities of self-restraint and the will to take personal responsibility for decisions. The problem comes when the benefit system removes the need for these values, thereby abolishing the need for moral fortitude. When morality is dropped as the guiding principle that keeps the poor from becoming the underclass, an individual's ability to make rational decisions on the basis of their best personal judgement (i.e. on the basis of their intelligence) may be all that is left.

Conclusion

I have assessed Murray's work on the underclass in the light of the updated trends and recent academic work. I have found that there *is* a growing underclass, and their modes of child rearing and their work patterns *are* increasingly alien to the rest of society. A modest prediction is that the weight of evidence will make obsolete disputes over the existence of an underclass or debates over the superiority of different forms of parenting. Instead the terms of academic debate will shift to the causes of the underclass and how to reduce it.

Table 1
How Over- or Under-represented Illegitimate Births are by Social Class

Social Class	Expected live births outside marriage jointly registered (1993)	Real Number of live births outside marriage jointly registered (1993)	% over-represented
I and II	31,000	28,900	-7
III Non-manual	27,800	12,000	-57
III Skilled Manual	63,000	66,300	+5
IV and V	34,600	49,200	+42
Total (excluding 'other')	156,400	156,400	

Table 2a
Response to the Statement 'I would pack in a job I didn't like even if there was no job to go to'

Class	Agree or Strongly Agree	Uncertain	Disagree or Strongly Disagree
	%	%	%
Underclass	39	21	40
Working-class	16	14	70

P<.0001

Table 2b
Response to the Statement 'Almost any job is better than none'

Class	Agree or Strongly Agree	Uncertain	Disagree or Strongly Disagree
	%	%	%
Underclass	47	9	44
Working-class	59	14	27

P<.0001

Table 3
Comparing the Birth Status of the Child by the Mean General Ability Score of the Mother

Birth Status of Child	Mean General Ability Score of Mother (out of 80)	Standard Deviation
Born Within Marriage	41.2	14.9
Illegitimate Child of Underclass Female	30.6	15.5
T-test	significance P<.001	t-value 6.19 and 1079df

Figure 1. Numbers of one-parent families, Great Britain

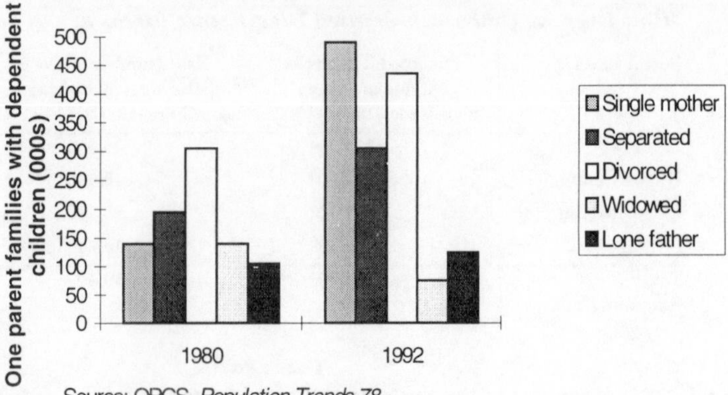

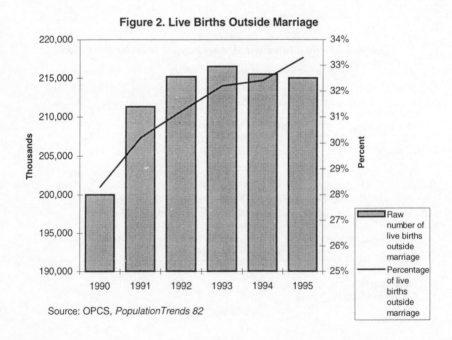

Source: OPCS, *Population Trends 78*

Figure 2. Live Births Outside Marriage

Source: OPCS, *PopulationTrends 82*

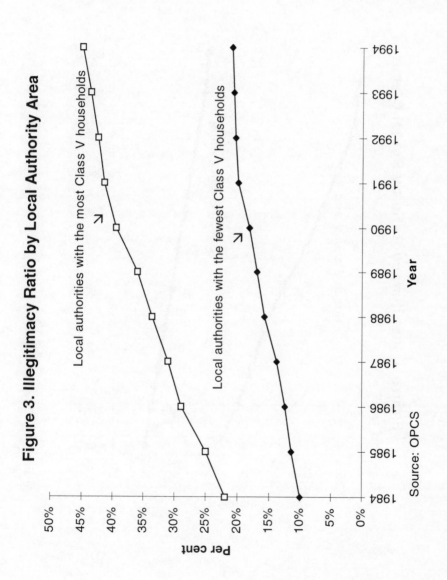

Figure 3. Illegitimacy Ratio by Local Authority Area

Local authorities with the most Class V households

Local authorities with the fewest Class V households

Source: OPCS

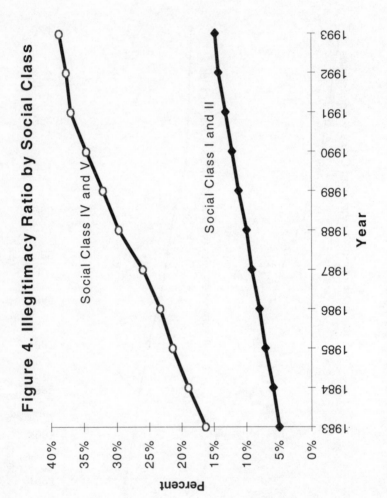

Figure 4. Illegitimacy Ratio by Social Class

Social Class IV and V

Social Class I and II

Percent

Year

Source: OPCS, *Key Birth Statistics 1993*.

Notes

1 All figures in this paragraph are derived from OPCS, *Social Trends 26*, 1996. 'Afro-Carribeans' consists of Caribbean, African and other Black people of non-mixed origin.

2 The 1995 figures are estimates based on figures for the first six months.

3 By 1993 there were only 210, 000 first marriages but 180, 000 divorces. *Social Trends 26*.

4 See her reply to Murray on pp. 156-60.

5 OPCS, *Key Birth Statistics 1993*.

6 By 1991 35 per cent of men were in classes I and II compared with 27.4 per cent in 1981. In classes IV and V, the figures were 23.5 per cent and 21 per cent respectively. OPCS Census data.

7 NCDS sweep 4 data was used to provide a rough guide to the proportions of fathers in each class when in their early twenties. The expected raw numbers were calculated by the formula $x*y/100$ where x = number of illegitimate births and y = % of men in the social class.

8 All statistics from OPCS, *Social Trends 26*.

9 See for example Magnet, M., *The Dream and the Nightmare*, New York: William Morrow, 1993. For a British account see Dennis, N., *Rising Crime and the Dismembered Family*, Choice in Welfare, No. 18, London: IEA Health and Welfare Unit, 1993.

10 Nickell, S. and Bell, B., 'The Collapse in Demand for the Unskilled and Unemployment Across the OECD', *Oxford Review of Economic Policy*, 1995, Vol. 11, No. 1, pp. 40-62.

11 Hills, J., *Inquiry into Income and Wealth*, Vol. 2. Joseph Rowntree Foundation, 1995.

12 Morgan, P., *Farewell to the Family? Public Policy and Family Breakdown in Britain and the USA*, London: IEA Health and Welfare Unit, 1995.

13 Krein, S. and Beller, A., 'Educational Attainment of Children from Single Parent Families: Differences by Exposure, Gender and Race', *Demography*, Vol. 25, No. 2, 1988.

14 Tripp, J. and Crockett, M., *Social Policy Research Findings,* No. 45, York: Joseph Rowntree Foundation, February 1994.

15 Wedge, P. and Essen, J., *Children in Adversity,* Pan Books, 1982. Pilling, D., *Escape From Disadvantage,* Falmer Press, 1990.

16 Dennis, N. and Erdos, G., *Families Without Fatherhood,* London: IEA Health and Welfare Unit, 1993.

17 For example, see Morris, L. and Irwin, S., 'Employment Histories and the Concept of the Underclass', *Sociology,* Vol. 26. No. 3, 1992.

18 To be considered members of the underclass they must have been out of the labour force for a total of at least 2.5 years by age 33 and have been on benefit and living in a council house (excluding those registered disabled).

19 Heath, A., in Smith, D.J. (ed.), *Understanding the Underclass,* London: Policy Studies Institute, 1991, p. 36; Morris, L. and Irwin, S., *op. cit.,* 1992, p. 418.

20 Scoring 4 points less than the working-class out of 80, and a full standard deviation less than the mean male score.

21 Kiernan, K., *Social Backgrounds and Post-Birth Experiences of Young Parents,* Social Policy Findings 80, Joseph Rowntree Foundation, 1995. She did not divide the sample according to marital status at the time of the child's birth, so included are 19 per cent of the sample who were married before conception.

22 Herrnstein, R. and Murray, C., *The Bell Curve,* New York: The Free Press, 1995, p. 179.